77 Creative Ways

Kids Can Serve

77 Creative Ways
Kids Can Serve

Sondra Clark

wesleyan
publishing
house

Indianapolis, Indiana

Copyright © 2008 by Sondra Clark
Published by Wesleyan Publishing House
Indianapolis, Indiana 46250
Printed in the United States of America
ISBN: 978-0-89827-363-2

Library of Congress Cataloging-in-Publication Data

Clark, Sondra.
  77 creative ways kids can serve / Sondra Clark.
    p. cm.
  Includes index.
  ISBN 978-0-89827-363-2
  1. Helping behavior--Religious aspects--Christianity. 2.
Change--Religious aspects--Christianity. I. Title. II. Title:
Seventy-seven creative ways to change your world.
  BV4647.H4C57 2008
  361.3'7--dc22
                              2007045564

The Web addresses (URLs) recommended throughout this book are solely offered as a resource to the reader. The citation of these websites does not in any way imply an endorsement on the part of the author or the publisher, nor do the author or publisher vouch for their content for the life of this book.

Contents

Introduction   7

Part 1: Service Projects with Animals   9

  1. Start a Butterfly Garden   10
  2. Make a Backyard Wildlife Sanctuary   12
  3. Buy a Goat   14
  4. Collect Tennis Balls for Animal Shelters   16
  5. Raise a Guide Dog for the Blind   18
  6. Take a Dog for a Walk   20
  7. Help Dogs Avoid Heatstroke   22
  8. Join Roots and Shoots   24

Part 2: Volunteer Ideas for Crafty Kids   27

  9. Give Away Easter Baskets   28
10. Decorate and Fill Art Bags for Ill Children   30
11. Bake Goodies for the Great American Bake Sale   32
12. Wrap for Charity   34
13. No-Sew Fleece Blankets   36
14. Prepare Birthday Bags for Children Living in Shelters   38
15. Give Giggle Bags   40
16. Make a Quilt That Gives More Than Warmth   42
17. Help Habitat for Humanity, Even if You Can't Swing a Hammer   44
18. Sell "Diamond" Pins   46
19. Fill Bedtime Snack Sacks   48
20. Design Funky Umbrellas   50
21. Celebrate "Stuffed with Hugs" Day   52
22. Raise Funds with Dinosaur-Teeth Necklaces   54

Part 3: Activities Connected with Recycling and the Environment   57

23. Recycle with a Recycling Carnival   58
24. Help Save the Rainforest   60
25. Plant a Tree   62
26. Help the Environment the Easy Way   64
27. Build a Rock Garden   66
28. Recycle at Home   68
29. Get a Passport in Time   70
30. Reduce, Reuse, Recycle   72
31. Be a Junior Forest Ranger   74
32. Pick Up Parks   76

Part 4: An Assortment of Tasks to Try   79

33. Put Together a Christmas Gift Bag   80
34. Give a GospelShoe   82
35. Promote Senior Computer Skills   84

36. Use Pen-and-Paper Power   86
37. Organize a Scrubbing Extravaganza   88
38. Volunteer with a Unique Camp   90
39. Help Special Athletes   92
40. Clean Baby Drool   94
41. Give Back to the Givers   96
42. Buy a "Kid"   98
43. Wear Jeans for a Cause   100
44. Put on a Show   102
45. Host a "Grandma and Me for Tea" Party   104
46. Start a "Do Something" Club   106
47. Fly Away with Airline Ambassadors   108
48. Help Ronald McDonald   110
49. Cut Your Hair for Locks of Love   112
50. Adopt an Angel   114
51. Bring Fresh Air to a Child   116
52. Create Senior Emergency Kits   118
53. Provide Entertainment for Children's Hospitals   120
54. Support the RandomKid Water Project   122
55. Help at Your Church   124
56. Go for the Glow   126
57. Give to Oprah's Angel Network   128
58. Make a Difference on Make A Difference Day   130
59. Hold a Spontaneous Car Wash   132
60. Get Involved with Doing Good Together   134
61. Help Children Escape Child Labor   136

Part 5: Suggestions for Collectors   139

62. Dress Up Dress-Up Boxes   140
63. Recycle Bibles   142
64. Swap Books   144
65. Collect Pajamas   146
66. Help Heavenly Hats   148
67. Glue Down Those Coins   150
68. Prepare Mini Hygiene Kits   152
69. Tap into a Dance Shoe Drive   154
70. Collect School Supplies for Kids   156
71. Score with a Sports Equipment Drive   158
72. Round up Extra Shoes   160
73. Give Stuffed Animals to Offer Comfort   162
74. Pack Up Backpacks for Foster Kids   164
75. Gather Hats for Homeless People   166
76. Collect Cell Phones for People in Need   168
77. Participate in the Pasta for Pennies Program   170

Index of Projects   172

V-O-L-U-N-T-E-E-R!   174

Introduction

I don't really remember my first volunteer experience. That's because I was still wearing diapers. An agency came to my mom and asked if I would volunteer to be in a video about cloth diapers. All I had to do was to sit in front of the camera (wearing cloth diapers) and play with toys while a person filmed me. Evidently it didn't go too well, because my mom says I kept crawling away and wouldn't sit where I was supposed to. Years went by and I began volunteering in more productive ways. One year, when I was nine, we volunteered to serve Easter dinner at a homeless shelter. When we arrived, the director said he had plenty of volunteers to pass out food. He asked if we'd come back in two hours and help clean up. That was the year I spent Easter cleaning toilets and scraping crusted food off plates.

My real passion for volunteering happened when I visited Kenya and Uganda as a twelve-year-old. As the tiny float plane lifted off the water and took me back to a major airport to go home, I knew I had two choices. I could go home and casually tell everyone about Africa while showing off the jewelry I bought, or I could use my experience to motivate myself to help change the world. I decided to show that kids can change the world.

By working with Childcare Worldwide, I've had the opportunity to travel to their programs in Africa, Peru, and Mexico. Then I came home and spoke to churches, schools, and service clubs, showing slides and asking people to sponsor a child in one of those countries. If a child has a sponsor in the United States, that child gets to go to school and break the cycle of poverty.

Volunteering isn't always easy. At times I'd speak to a school where the kids whispered, squirmed, and made it obvious they weren't interest in volunteering. I once was scheduled to do an hour-long radio interview when I had food poisoning. (I laid on the floor by the toilet while being interviewed.) Yet I saw my volunteer efforts make a difference in the lives of children in developing countries. I started a program called "FUN With A FUTURE" where I collected a thousand Frisbee-type discs (for FUN) and ten thousand pencils and five thousand toothbrushes (for the FUTURE) to help kids I met. Many kids in Africa had to share a pencil, so they were thrilled to have their very own pencil.

Now I'm involved with Soles4Souls, an agency that wants to impact as many lives as possible with the gift of shoes. They ask people to collect gently worn shoes or donate money for new shoes. Then Soles4Souls gets those shoes to needy people around the world. I just got back from Guatemala, where I passed out shoes to children in remote villages. It amazed me how some of these kids walked around with worn-out shoes, encrusted with dirt and three sizes too big. They had no other choice but to wear old shoes because their families could barely make enough money to live, let alone buy shoes. I helped the kids take off their old shoes. Most kids had filthy feet covered by socks with huge holes. The kids were thrilled to get new flip-flops. Many put the shoes on right away, because they had been barefoot. It was great seeing their smiles as they walked home with new shoes.

You don't have to go to Africa or Guatemala to volunteer. So many opportunities exist in your own community. How about asking a Sunday school teacher if you can help decorate her bulletin board? Did a neighbor sprain his ankle? Offer to take his dog for a walk. Still need more ideas? Look through this book. There should be some project that matches your skills and interests. Just remember, kids can change the world.

Happy volunteering!
Sondra

Part 1

Service Projects with Animals

Most kids like animals, whether cuddling your own cat or seeing lions at the zoo. Here are some ways to volunteer with a number of possibilities that have to do with dogs, cats, and even butterflies!

Start a
Butterfly Garden

No, you're not going to grow butterflies. Did you know you can attract butterflies by planting flowers? Butterflies are drawn to certain flowers with clusters of blossoms. Try this great project that involves planting a butterfly garden to create a place for people to watch colorful butterflies fluttering around.

Here's What You'll Need

Packets of seeds or potted plants

An area to plant flowers

Shovels and rakes

Hoses or buckets of water

Follow These Easy Steps

1. Find a place that would enjoy a butterfly garden. You could contact a senior center, preschool, or Head Start program. Maybe your school has a patch of land you can transform into a butterfly garden. All you need is an area of dirt about two feet by three feet.

2. Buy an assortment of seeds or plants that attract butterflies. These include Queen Anne's lace, yarrow, snapdragons, black-eyed Susan, sunflowers, and—get this—a butterfly bush. Butterflies like bunches of flowers close together, rather than spread out in neat, even rows.

3. Go to your location and prepare the soil. Rake out large rocks and clumps of dirt. Follow the directions on the seed packets to plant the seeds at the correct depth. Water well during the first few weeks to get the roots growing. After the flowers are blooming, add a shallow container of water for the butterflies to drink. Add a smooth rock or two to the container so the butterflies have a place to land. Make a plan as to how you'll keep the butterfly garden watered and free from weeds. Soon people walking by will enjoy a variety of butterflies fluttering around the area.

More than 700 species of butterflies fly around the world.

Get More Information

Want to know more about butterflies? Check out www.thebutterflysite.com for fun information about these colorful flying insects.

Make a Backyard Wildlife Sanctuary

Wouldn't it be great to live in the jungle where all sorts of exotic animals roamed in your backyard? You probably can't have lions and elephants prowling around your suburban house, but you can set up a modified wildlife sanctuary. Did you know any family with a grassy or wooded backyard can be a habitat manager? There's more wildlife around your house than you know. Do you have hummingbirds zipping by your window? Any spider webs stretched between branches on a bush? See? You are in close proximity to wildlife. The National Wildlife Federation (NWF) has a program to help you certify your yard as a "Backyard Wildlife Sanctuary."

Here's What You'll Need

A variety of birdhouses, bat houses, a birdbath or garden pond, trees, and shrubs (Don't worry, you don't need all those items.)

$5, $15, or $20, depending on how much information you want and

Follow These Easy Steps

1. Read the step-by-step information on the NWF website (www.nwf.org/backyard) to make sure your yard is "wildlife friendly" or to make any adjustments or additions.

2. Download the Application for Certification on the NWF website.

3. Fill out the form and send it with $15 to the address indicated. (You can also complete the process online.)

4. Within four to six weeks, you'll get a personalized certificate, an NWF membership, a year's subscription to National Wildlife magazine, an e-newsletter subscription, and your name listed in NWF's national registry of certified habitats.

5. Get to work creating a backyard wildlife sanctuary and helping animals that lived in your neighborhood long before you did.

One of the most common animals you'll find in a backyard are squirrels. There are over 1,6500 types of squirrels.

Get More Information

If you're a resident of either Washington or North Carolina, you can also be certified by your state (for $5 more). You can get more details at http://wdfw.wa.gov/wlm/backyard for Washington and www.ncwildlifefederation.org for North Carolina.

Buy a Goat

Do you like animals? Here's a unique way to help families in developing countries to have a better life. Buy them a cow . . . or a sheep . . . or a water buffalo. You can even buy them a flock of chicks. Heifer International works to end world hunger and save the earth. Instead of providing hungry families with a nonrenewable source of food, Heifer International provides a "living loan" of an animal. The family's health and standard of living is improved by owning the animal. They might benefit from milk from a cow or goat, eggs from chickens, meat from rabbits, draft power from water buffalo, or wool from llamas.

Here's What You'll Need

Money

Follow These Easy Steps

1. Heifer International has twenty-eight animals you can choose from. Here are some sample prices:

- A flock of chicks: $20—One hen can provide a family with two hundred eggs per year.
- Honeybees: $30—Families eat and sell the honey and sell the beeswax. The bees pollinate fruits and vegetables so they grow better.

- One sheep: $120—People can use the wool to sell or make their own clothes. The sheep manure is used as fertilizer.
- A "Milk Menagerie": $1,000—This buys four animals that produce milk, such as one heifer, two goats, and one water buffalo. Families drink the milk and sell the extra.

2. Figure out your budget, then use the money to buy an animal. Some kids have asked friends and relatives to donate money in place of birthday presents. You'll always remember the birthday where you bought a flock of chicks and a goat.

The milk from a water buffalo can be used to make yogurt and mozzarella cheese.

3. If you want to buy a more expensive animal, get together with a group and pool your money. One family, instead of buying each other individual Christmas presents, chipped in $20 each and bought a pig and two goats.

4. Check out the www.readtofeed.org website. It has lots of information on how you can raise money for Heifer International with your class or youth group. The program offers free resources with plenty of ideas.

Get More Information

The Heifer International website (www.heifer.org) has all the information you need to help you select an animal.

Collect Tennis Balls for Animal Shelters

Does your dog love chasing balls you throw to him? Dogs thrive with love, attention, and exercise. But not all dogs get that personal care. Abandoned dogs living in shelters don't get to play with an owner in a park. You can bring a little fun back to dogs in a shelter by collecting used tennis balls. Volunteers and staff use the balls to interact with the dogs. Other times, dogs get tennis balls in their pens to help break the boredom of being confined all day.

Here's What You'll Need

Transportation to various locations to collect tennis balls

A box or tub to collect the balls

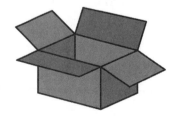

Follow These Easy Steps

1. Tennis balls lose their bounce and can't be used for playing tennis after a certain amount of time. So, you'll be able to find places that normally would throw away these used, "flat" tennis balls.

2. Contact the local tennis club and ask if they have old tennis balls they don't need. Offer to come by with a few boxes labeled "Donate old tennis balls to dogs at the Humane Society." This encourages players to donate the balls instead of casually tossing them in a trash can.

3. Also, if your school has a tennis team, ask the coach to announce you are collecting old tennis balls. Call the tennis coaches at

high schools in your area and explain your project. They can ask players to donate used balls.

4. Contact your local parks and recreation department and talk to an athletic supervisor. Many parks have tennis courts. Be bold and ask if groundskeepers can collect used balls from trash cans and save them for you to pick up.

5. Arrange a time to pick up collected balls.

6. After you've collected the tennis balls, call the shelter to arrange a drop-off time. Ask if you can also get a tour of the facility. Maybe another volunteer opportunity will come up as you walk through the shelter. For example, many shelters need old newspapers for the puppy pens. See, you can change the world by collecting newspapers and tennis balls to make lots of dogs happy.

In 2006 the most popular breed of dog was the Labrador retriever.

Get More Information

The website www.pets911.com has links that give phone numbers for shelters across the country. Call a shelter in your area to see if they need extra tennis balls for the dogs.

Raise a Guide Dog for the Blind

At one time or another you probably pestered your parents to buy you a puppy (even if your family already has a dog). Here's a unique way to be involved with a dog that isn't your own. Some people with vision problems rely on seeing eye dogs to be their eyes to the world. These specially trained dogs need to grow from puppies in a friendly family home. That's where you come in. With your parents' approval, see about raising a puppy in preparation for being a guide dog for the blind. Your main job is to get the puppy used to everyday situations like riding in a car, being around kids, and going to the grocery store. See, you can change the world by doing everyday things.

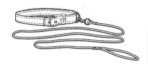

Here's What You'll Need

A dog bed

Dog leash, collar, bowls, etc.

Money for dog food

You need to be at least nine years old.

You must live in Arizona, California, Colorado, Idaho, Nevada, Oregon, Utah, or Washington.

Follow These Easy Steps

1. If your parents agree to help you get involved in raising a guide dog, contact the Canine Community Programs office at Guide Dogs for the Blind at 800-295-4050.

2. Set a time for the local representative to interview you. They want to make sure you have a safe place for the puppy to live. They'll also check that the puppy has a bed indoors and someone available to supervise the puppy during the day. (Puppies have a way of chewing good shoes and having accidents on living room carpet.)

3. Your parents will have to fill out applications and other paperwork.

4. Many 4-H clubs are connected with the guide dog program. See if you can join a local club and meet other kids involved in this volunteer project.

As a puppy raiser, you're invited to the dogs' graduation ceremony, where you'll hand your puppy over to his or her new blind owners. Because of your efforts, that person will have a well-trained dog and the ability to go to work or school.

5. If accepted as an official puppy raiser, you'll receive an eight-week-old puppy who stays with you until he or she is thirteen to eighteen months old. It's up to your family to pay for the dog food.

6. You'll learn specific training ideas by attending training workshops and guide dog puppy clubs.

7. The organization sponsors Puppy Fun Days as a way to thank you for volunteering to raise a dog.

Get More Information

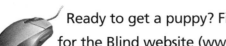

Ready to get a puppy? Find out more on the Guide Dogs for the Blind website (www.guidedogs.com).

Take a Dog for a Walk

6

Do you love dogs? Does your heart melt when you see a cute puppy with floppy ears and wagging tail? Sadly, many pets get abandoned, especially as they get older and lose their cuteness. Some owners don't realize dogs need consistent exercise and training. Unwanted pets often end up in animal shelters. Shelters rely on volunteers to give dogs exercise by walking them or playing catch in an exercise pen. If you love working with animals, this is a great chance for you to interact with dogs that need attention. Abused dogs need personal attention so they can get comfortable around humans to help their chances of being adopted. They also need to burn all that energy by taking a walk or catching a ball.

Here's What You'll Need

Transportation to the animal shelter

Follow These Easy Steps

1. Check out the Website www.pets911.com, and go to the link "volunteer." Type your zip code and find a list of shelters where you can help. Many communities also have private animal shelters looking for volunteer walkers.

2. Contact the animal shelter to explain your desire to walk or exercise dogs. Ask if you need an adult with you. Some require kids under sixteen to volunteer with an adult if they plan on leaving the shelter to take a dog for a walk. In most cases the shelter gives you one or two dogs on a leash and suggests a walking path close to the shelter. Tell your mom or dad this is a great way to get exercise while doing volunteer work.

3. If the shelter needs people to play with dogs in an exercise pen, invite a friend or two to help toss Frisbees and balls. You can make volunteering a fun group activity. Many times the dogs just need personal attention. Spend a lively afternoon playing catch with dogs and hanging out with friends.

If you go to camp, why can't your dog? Get your family to spend a week at Camp Gone to the Dogs (www.camp-gone-tothe-dogs.com), where you and your dog do all sorts camp activities together.

Get More Information

If you want more ways to help animals in shelters, check out the website of the National Humane Society (http://www.hsus.org). The site includes facts and information about shelters and ways to help end animal cruelty.

Help Dogs Avoid Heatstroke

7

Have you ever gotten into a car on a hot day and felt a blast of heat as you opened the door? Even on a moderately warm day of 73 degrees, the temperature inside the car can reach 120 in less than 30 minutes. On a hot day of 90 degrees, the temperature inside a car quickly reaches 160. Unfortunately, many people think they can roll a window down a tiny bit and leave their dog in the car. Here's a way to volunteer by educating people about the dangers of leaving dogs in parked cars.

Here's What You'll Need

Flyers to put on car windows

Follow These Easy Steps

1. The Humane Society of the United States (HSUS) has posters and flyers available to help educate people about the dangers of leaving pets in the car. You can order them (posters: 10 for $3 or 25 for $5; flyers: 50 for $3) from

HSUS/Hot Cars
2100 L St., NW
Washington, DC 20037

2. Keep a few flyers with you to place on a car windshield when you see a dog inside a locked car.

3. You also can design your own flyer informing people about the dangers of leaving a dog inside a car on even a warm day. Try writing the note from the dog's perspective, such as "Dear Owner: Did you know that cars get *very* hot, even with the windows cracked open? Please don't leave me in this car again. I don't sweat like you do, so I have no way to cool down. Love, Your Dog." Print these cards on your computer and keep them in your family car. If you go to a store or restaurant with your parents and see a dog inside a hot car, leave the flyer on the dog owner's windshield as a gentle reminder.

The hottest temperature ever recorded in the United States was on July 10, 1913. It got to 134 degrees at Greenland Ranch, Death Valley, California.

4. An easy way to reach a large number of people is to write a letter to the editor of your local newspaper. Look in the paper for the mailing address and format. Most editors request letters stay under four hundred words. Write a short, clear letter giving a few facts to inform people they could be jeopardizing their dogs' health. Most people like having their dog with them but forget how quickly cars get to a sweltering temperature.

Get More Information

You'll find lots of great information on dogs at www.dogs.about.com. You can find specific information on heat stroke at www.dogs.about.com/cs/generalcare/a/heatstroke.

8   Join Roots and Shoots

When I was twelve years old I became obsessed with Jane Goodall and her work with chimpanzees. I painted leaves on my bedroom walls to look like a jungle. I even had my dad put in huge bamboo poles and netting to make it look like a research center.

I was inspired by the ambition of this woman to learn and study chimpanzees in the jungle. One of my favorite Jane Goodall quotes is "Do the small things. Pick up the phone or write a letter, and never let anyone ever tell you it doesn't make a difference." That's also true with volunteering. Even a small activity makes a difference.

Jane took her ideas of volunteering to another level and started Roots and Shoots, an organization that gives kids tools to create their own volunteer projects.

Follow These Easy Steps

1. Roots and Shoots has many ways to get involved. The easiest is to log on to their website and type in your zip code. Their directory shows established clubs in your area. Then all you have to do is call and ask to join. The trained leader will make you feel welcome and get you involved.

2. If there's no club in your area, find an adult to help you start one. Get some of your friends together who are concerned with saving animals and the environment. Once an adult registers your club, Roots and Shoots sends all sorts of helpful information to help you carry out projects.

3. Don't worry if you can't think of an activity. Their project database has ideas ranging from park clean-up to building birdhouses to canned food drives to giving speeches to school groups. One club encouraged people in their community to use cloth bags when shopping. This reduced the amount of plastic and paper bags most of us use without thinking.

4. If you've recently done a fund-raiser, consider donating money to Roots and Shoots. Your money helps their chimpanzee rehabilitation centers as well as their efforts to restore the African habitat.

5. Are you over fourteen? Then you can apply to be on the Roots and Shoots Leadership Council. You'll communicate with other teens on specific projects dealing with animals or the environment.

There are thought to be 175,000 chimpanzees remaining in the wild, but their numbers are decreasing at an alarming rate as their habitats are destroyed.

Get More Information

 Check out the Roots and Shoots website (www.rootsandshoots.org).

Part 2

Volunteer Ideas
for Crafty Kids

Many kids like making arts and crafts projects where they get to be creative and paint or decorate things. Check out these activities if you like doing crafty projects to help other people.

Give Away Easter Baskets

9

Every Easter, my parents hand me a clue for the traditional "Easter basket treasure hunt." That clue leads to another, and another . . . and another. Each year the hunt and the clues become more complex until I find my Easter basket. My basket has been hidden in the shower, the car, the oven, and even on the roof. Even though I'm seventeen, I look forward to my hunt and the basket at the end.

But not every kid gets to wake to an Easter basket. Kids in homeless shelters miss out on chocolate bunnies and the squishy Peeps we all love.

Here's What You'll Need

Variety of Easter baskets (If you don't want to collect Easter baskets, decorate paper lunch bags and call them "Easter bags.")

Plastic "grass" or other filler

Assortment of pencils, socks, combs, toothbrushes

Candy and chocolate bunnies

Follow These Easy Steps

1. Ask an adult to help you find a homeless shelter or church that is providing an Easter dinner that includes children. Often, your local newspaper will list details about churches that invite homeless and low-income people to a special Easter dinner.

2. Call and ask if you can donate Easter baskets.

3. Check your closets for last year's Easter baskets. You probably have a few extra tucked away in storage. Many garage sales sell regular baskets and Easter baskets for fifty cents. Ask a few friends or relatives to donate empty baskets, as well as basket stuffers.

4. Fill as many baskets as possible with the plastic grass and the goodies. The baskets don't have to be filled totally with candy. Include a few items like small puzzles, books, pencils, or granola bars. Of course, you'll add some candy to provide that sweet touch to the basket.

5. Have an adult take you to deliver the baskets. You might see if you can help serve food at the Easter dinner.

6. Here's an additional tip, but you have to plan in advance. On the day after Easter, many stores sell Easter items at 50–75 percent off. Buy as many items as you can afford (not candy, though). This is a great chance to stock up on Easter crossword puzzles, bookmarks, pencils, and other novelties. Then remember where you stored these bargains for next Easter. See, kids can change the world by shopping after-holiday sales.

Seventy-six percent of people eat the ears off a chocolate Easter bunny first.

Decorate and Fill Art Bags for Ill Children

10

Here's a way to use your artistic abilities to help bring fun to sick kids. Decorate canvas bags and fill them with new art supplies. The bags can be donated to a children's hospital so a child not feeling well has a way to pass the time.

Here's What You'll Need

Plain cloth or canvas bags

Fabric paint

Permanent markers

Scraps of ribbon, lace, extra buttons, etc.

Fabric glue

Scissors

Assorted art supplies like paper, crayons, stickers, etc.

Follow These Easy Steps

1. Call a local hospital to ask if they would like to receive a few art-supply bags. If they say yes, you're ready to do this volunteer project.

2. Start collecting art supplies. Maybe your mom will let you buy crayons, construction paper, or glue each time she goes grocery shopping. If you buy one item at a time, you won't break your budget. Dollar stores are great places to buy inexpensive art supplies. Our dollar store has a huge supply of rubber stamps and ink pads.

3. Go to a nearby craft store with an adult and ask to talk to the manager. Explain how you are decorating and filling art bags to donate to a children's hospital. Be bold and ask if the store will donate canvas bags, fabric glue, or art supplies. Sometimes the store will offer you a discount if they can't make a donation.

4. Another way to get the bags is from a company called Innovative Greetings. Their website (www.ingreetings.com) sells a variety of reasonably priced plain bags. Some bags are only 65¢.

5. After you have a few plain bags, get creative and start decorating. Fabric paint is a great way to decorate with colorful designs. If you don't have craft paint, use permanent markers.

6. Embellish the bags with ribbon or buttons you have around the house. It's fun to glue on a colorful button, then use paint or markers to draw petals around the button. You now have a three-dimensional flower.

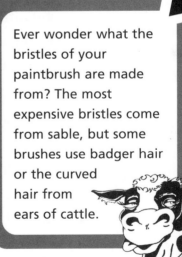

Ever wonder what the bristles of your paintbrush are made from? The most expensive bristles come from sable, but some brushes use badger hair or the curved hair from ears of cattle.

7. Make sure the paint is dry before you fill the bag with supplies.

8. Call your contact at the hospital and arrange for a time to deliver the finished bags.

Bake Goodies for the Great American Bake Sale

11

Bake sales have always been a traditional way to raise money for a cause. People gladly pay a little extra for a gooey brownie or chocolate cupcake, knowing the money goes to a good cause. One organization took ordinary bake sales to the next level by organizing a *gigantic* bake sale. The Great American Bake Sale has raised millions of dollars to help end childhood hunger. The money earned from thousands of bake sales across the country is distributed by Share Our Strength, which gives the funds to local agencies in your state.

Here's What You'll Need

Table and tablecloth

Paper plates and clear plastic wrap

Assorted baked goods

Cash box

Change for sales

Latex gloves

Signs

Follow These Easy Steps

1. Go to the Great American Bake Sale website (http://gabs.strength.org) and ask your parents to register your bake sale. It's an easy form that won't take long.

2. The Great American Bake Sale suggests you have your sale between May 19 and August 31. Pick a date and location to hold the sale. Try to find a busy store or office where plenty of people walk by. Do one of your parents work in an office where you could sell baked items in the afternoon when everyone is craving a treat? Ask your dance teacher if you can set up a table with baked goods at the studio. Parents and kids are sure to buy something. If you attend a church, ask the pastor if you can sell goodies after the morning service. People are always hungry after church.

3. Try to get family and friends to volunteer to bake items. Does Grandma make a yummy coconut cake? Is your dad an expert at making Rice Krispies treats? Ask them to bake the items and deliver them the day of your sale.

4. On the day of the big event, use the gloves (for health reasons) while wrapping the cookies, brownies, fudge, slices of cake, or whatever in plastic wrap.

5. Clearly price each item.

6. Make a sign telling people where the money is going. Some people might give extra money as a donation.

The Immaculate Baking Company baked a cookie that was 102 feet in diameter, weighed about 37,000 pounds, and used 30,000 eggs and 6,000 pounds of chocolate.

7. Have a cash box and extra dollar bills and coins to make change.

8. When you have finished your sale, give the cash to your parents and ask them to write a check for that amount to Share Our Strength. Mail the check to the address you received when you registered online.

Get More Information

Check out the Great American Bake Sale website (http://gabs.strength.org) for details. More than 91 percent of the money collected from all the bake sales goes to organizations fighting hunger.

Wrap for Charity

I guess if you didn't see this title in print you'd think I said "Rap for Charity," and you'd have to learn some fancy rap routine. Actually, this project involves wrapping presents, not rapping songs. This is a fun way to raise money for a charity and be creative with your friends while providing a service. During the holiday season, offer to wrap presents for people too busy or unable to wrap their own presents.

Here's What You'll Need

Wrapping paper

Ribbons and bows

Scissors

Tape

Signs

A box with a "Donations Accepted" sign attached

Table and chairs

Follow These Easy Steps

1. Several weeks ahead, find a store, senior center, or office building close to an area where people shop. Get permission to set up your wrapping station. Bookstores are a great place to set up, because books are easy to wrap.

2. Ask family and friends for donations of wrapping paper and bows. Maybe your mom bought several rolls of wrapping paper at last year's after-Christmas sale. Have a good supply of ribbons and bows. Check that you have several pairs of scissors and rolls of tape. Try to have gift bags and tissue paper to wrap items with weird shapes. It's easier to put a teddy bear in a gift bag than to wrap it with paper.

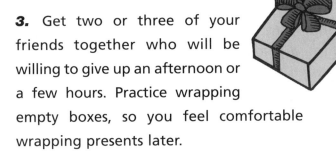

3. Get two or three of your friends together who will be willing to give up an afternoon or a few hours. Practice wrapping empty boxes, so you feel comfortable wrapping presents later.

4. On the day of the event, set your table in a noticeable place. Put up signs saying "Free Gift Wrapping." Then get ready to tie ribbons and add colorful bows. Be sure to smile at people as they bring you their presents. Some people get stressed out shopping.

5. At the end of your wrapping session, clean up the area and thank the store manager for letting you be there.

Here's a spin on this idea:
Many seniors have trouble tying bows and wrapping packages. Offer to go to a senior center to wrap presents without asking for a donation. Do it to help add holiday spirit.

6. Give the money you received from donations to your favorite charity.

13 No-Sew Fleece Blankets

Did you have a favorite blanket growing up? Does it have tattered edges and a name like Buddy or Blankey? A soft, comfy blanket gives warmth and comfort to people. Now you can make and give a no-sew blanket to someone who needs a little warmth.

Here's What You'll Need

1 ½ yard of fleece fabric if you want a baby blanket

2 yards of fleece fabric if you want a teen or adult blanket

Sharp scissors

Follow These Easy Steps

1. Ask your parent to take you to the fabric or craft store to pick out the material. There are so many cool patterns of fleece; the hardest part of this project will be picking out which pattern you like best. The blankets turn out great if you get one side with a pattern and the other a solid color that matches.

2. When you get home, have an adult help you use the sharpest scissors in your house. This would be a great craft to do with a parent.

3. Lay your fabrics, one on top of the other, "right" sides out, on a flat surface. Make sure they match up and all the wrinkles are smoothed out. Cut off the selvege (machine-sewn) edges. Cut a four-inch square out of each corner. Now make a four-inch cut from one edge toward the center of the fabrics. Make four-inch cuts every two inches all around the four edges of the fabric. Your fabric will look like it has fringes. Start at one corner and tie each "pair" of strips in two double knots. (That way, they'll be sure to stay together in the wash.) Make the knots as far from the edge as you can, since you want the blanket to be "fringed" when you're done. Tie knots all the way around the blanket.

4. It may take a while, so you might want to pop in your favorite CD or video while you work. I usually do it while watching TV. This is also a great project to work on with a few friends.

5. You'll soon have a great blanket you can donate to a nursing home, children's hospital, homeless shelter, or wherever you choose. The fleece is super soft and washes well in the washing machine.

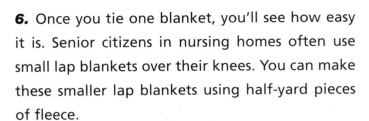

Some polar fleece material is made from recycled plastic bottles.

6. Once you tie one blanket, you'll see how easy it is. Senior citizens in nursing homes often use small lap blankets over their knees. You can make these smaller lap blankets using half-yard pieces of fleece.

Prepare Birthday Bags for Children Living in Shelters

Think about your last birthday party. You probably went ice skating, saw a movie, or had a theme party with a group of friends. You opened a pile of presents, all wrapped in colorful paper with big bows. Later, you dug into a cake loaded with sugary frosting.

Have you ever thought that some kids don't get to celebrate their birthdays with parties, presents, and cakes? If children live in a shelter, it's hard for their parents to have the money and resources to plan a birthday party. Here's how you can help.

Here's What You'll Need

Large paper grocery bags

Markers, stickers, glitter, etc.

Assorted party supplies like balloons, streamers, Happy Birthday signs, etc.

New toy or craft item

Packaged cake mix and canned frosting

Birthday candles

Follow These Easy Steps

1. Have an adult help you call a local homeless shelter. Tell them your plans to put together birthday kits for children at their center. They'll tell you the best time to deliver the bags. Get three or four paper grocery bags and decorate them with colorful pictures and stickers. Be sure to write "Happy Birthday!" in bold letters.

2. Keep the bags in an easy-to-see place, and start filling them. Ask your parents to buy an extra package of cake mix or a box of candles whenever they go to the store. Add those items to the bags. If a mother at the shelter has the supplies to make a cake, she can most likely use the shelter kitchen to do the baking.

3. Look around your house for birthday supplies. If you find extra balloons or a new package of streamers, put those items in the bags.

4. Make sure each bag contains a new present for the child. Maybe you can use some of your birthday money to buy the gifts. Wrap the present and make sure to identify the gift on the outside of your decorated bags. You might attach a note that says "For a preschool girl" or "Birthday bag for elementary-age boy," depending on the gift. You also could give a general gift that kids of all ages would like, such as new markers and construction paper.

In 2005 Sara Lee bakery assembled the world's largest birthday cake. A thousand volunteers spread 40,000 pounds of frosting on the cake. Now that's a big cake!

5. After the bags are full, call the shelter to let them know you are ready to deliver the bags. Ask an adult to drive you to the shelter. You're guaranteed to make some kids' birthdays extra special.

Give Giggle Bags

Have you ever been in the hospital? Many times even spending a few days in a hospital can be boring—it doesn't take long to get tired of watching TV and DVDs. Bring some joy and fun to kids staying in the hospital by making Giggle Bags.

Here's What You'll Need

Lunch bags

Markers and other things to decorate the bags

Small items from the dollar store

Whoopee cushions or other "gag" toys

Follow These Easy Steps

1. Call a local children's hospital and ask to talk to the volunteer coordinator. That person will tell you if they can use the Giggle Bags. He or she will also tell you if there are certain items not to include. Some hospitals have rules about allowing latex balloons in the children's wing because of the possibility of choking on a popped balloon.

2. Ask your parents if they would be willing to help you buy things from the dollar store to put in the Giggle Bags. You can do extra chores if you want to earn more money to help. You can even write a letter to the manager of the store to tell him or her what you are doing and ask if the store would be willing to donate items.

3. Decide if you want to make the bags specifically for a girl or boy or general enough for either. That will help you as you buy items.

4. Go to the store and buy silly items. You can buy bubbles, puzzles, handheld games, or even a whoopee cushion. Perhaps you have a book in good condition you've read that you want to donate. Think about things you would like if you were stuck in a hospital bed.

5. When you get all the giggle items home, take the brown lunch bags and decorate them with smiley faces, hearts, and stars. Make sure to label them "Giggle Bags." Put the items in the bags, and tape them closed.

6. Make a simple card that says something like, "Here are some fun things to keep you busy. Enjoy." Tape the card to the bag.

7. Ask a parent to take you to a hospital to drop off the Giggle Bags. Maybe the volunteer coordinator will let you deliver them. Then you can see how happy they make kids.

It's good to laugh. Laughing 100 times is as good for you as riding 15 minutes on an exercise bike.

Get More Information

Many hospitals with children's wings hire people called "child life specialists." These people look for ways to minimize the stress children feel when they're in the hospital. They can offer suggestions about what to add to your Giggle Bags.

Make a Quilt That Gives More Than Warmth

16

More Than Warmth is an organization looking for volunteers to make quilts for children in need. So far ten thousand kids have volunteered to make more than a thousand quilts. This is a great group project for a Sunday school class or scout troop. Judith Biondo Meeker, the founder of the group, sends quilts to Ghana, Africa, India, China, and Afghanistan. Her program is an educational project for students of all ages to learn about world cultures and to feel compassion for others from different cultural backgrounds.

Here's What You'll Need

Fabric markers (available at any craft store)

One yard of muslin

Sharp scissors

Ruler or tape measure

Padded envelope or flat box to ship quilt squares

Paper and pen to write a letter

Follow These Easy Steps

1. Have an adult help you cut the muslin into eleven-and-a-half-inches per square. Use a tape measure or ruler to help get the correct size. It's easiest to cut fabric when it's on a flat surface like a table.

2. Use fabric markers to decorate each square with a colorful design. It's fun to have several people decorate the squares. That's where your Sunday school class or soccer team can help. Draw pictures of "positive" things like rainbows and butterflies. Many these children live in areas of war and poverty, so your picture should be uplifting.

3. The More Than Warmth website's cultural resources page (http://www.morethanwarmth.org/resources.html) has pictures to guide you and give you an idea how the completed quilts look. After you send your quilt squares to them, a professional completes the quilt.

Leona Tennyson and her friends made the world's largest historical quilt. It shows every county in North Dakota with a different colored fabric and covers almost one third of an acre. Think about that while you make your quilt squares.

4. The More Than Warmth Organization encourages everyone working on a quilt to write a letter to the child who will receive the finished quilt. This adds a personal touch and lets a child in a stressful environment know some other child is thinking about him or her.

5. If possible, send a donation to help cover the cost of shipping the quilt overseas.

Get More Information

Send your quilt squares to

More Than Warmth
1115 Williamson County Road
Fairview, TN 37062

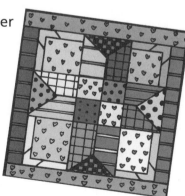

Help Habitat for Humanity, Even if You Can't Swing a Hammer

You've probably heard about Habitat for Humanity. They get volunteers to help build homes for needy people. While you have to be at least sixteen to actually help build a house, you can make a difference by joining the Habitat for Humanity Youth Programs (http://www.habitat.org/youthprograms). These activities are designed for five- to twenty-five-year-olds who want to do something to help eliminate poverty.

Here's What You'll Need

Supplies vary, depending on the project.

Follow These Easy Steps

1. Contact your local Habitat for Humanity office. Go on their website (www.habitat.org), and you'll find a place to put in your zip code. A contact person and phone number will pop up so you can get information about youth programs in your area.

2. Like doing crafts? The Habitat for Humanity youth programs offer a card-making template on their website. It's designed for five- to nine-year-olds to make cards and publicize the need for people to have decent housing.

3. The youth website also has a pattern to make a paper house so you can send it to lawmakers and important people in your community. Make the paper house and write a letter encouraging the mayor or governor to help eliminate homelessness. Letters make a big impact.

welcome home!

4. Habitat for Humanity's website also has directions on making a key holder. This makes a great welcoming gift so the new owners have a holder for their new house key. The website also includes games, crossword puzzles, and fun activities related to how you can help the homeless.

5. When a house is completed, Habitat for Humanity needs help planning the celebration. Offer to put up balloons or streamers. Perhaps you could make a fancy Welcome Home sign for the front door. Check with the site coordinator to see whether you can bring cookies or a cake to the celebration.

Habitat has built more than 225,000 houses around the world, providing more than 1,000,000 people in more than 3,000 communities with safe, decent, affordable shelter.

Get More Information

The Habitat for Humanity website (www.habitat.org/youthprograms) has more ideas on how kids can volunteer.

Sell "Diamond" Pins

Sometimes you need to make money to carry out your volunteer project. Here's a fun idea that catches people's interest because they wonder how you could be selling "diamond" pins. Well, actually it's a joke. Instead of selling a two-carat diamond worth millions of dollars, you are selling a "dime and pin." Get it?

Here's What You'll Need

Safety pins

Dimes

Glue

Glue gun if an adult is close by to help

One-inch- or two-inch-wide ribbon, assorted colors

Scissors

Follow These Easy Steps

1. Before you make and sell these pins, decide where the money will go. People are more likely to buy the pins if they know the money is going to a good cause. If you have a brochure or other information on your project, that also helps in getting people to contribute. You could make a small label that says, "Purchase a Diamond Pin to help buy books for missionaries in Peru."

2. Cut the ribbon into pieces about four inches long.

3. Close the safety pin and slip one end of the ribbon through the pin to make the ends meet. This makes it look like a badge.

4. Glue the underside of the top ribbon so it stays in place.

5. Spread a bit of glue on the center of the ribbon by the safety pin.

6. Place a dime, face side up, on the glue.

7. You now have a "Diamond Pin" someone can actually wear.

8. Try making the pins with red, white, and blue ribbons and use the money for a project to benefit men and women in the military.

9. Sell your pins to relatives, teachers, and friends. See if your parents will take them to work and sell them to co-workers as a gag gift. Many people find they sell well for $1 each. Collect your money and donate it to your selected volunteer program.

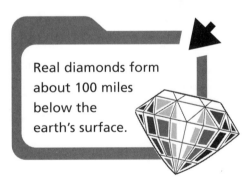

Real diamonds form about 100 miles below the earth's surface.

Get More Information

Looking for a great place to get inexpensive ribbon, safety pins, pom-poms, glitter, felt, foam, and other craft supplies? Order a free S&S Worldwide catalog full of craft supplies and craft kits from their website (www.ssww.com).

Fill Bedtime Snack Sacks

Do you like having a bedtime snack? I know I do. But there are kids living in homeless shelters who don't get to have a treat like we do. Here's a chance to give kids a little snack before going to bed.

Here's What You'll Need

Brown lunch bags

Markers, crayons

Stickers, glitter, etc.

Juice box

Granola bars, raisins, etc.

Small toys like you get in a fast-food kids' meals

Follow These Easy Steps

1. You'll probably need your parents' help for this project. Ask if they'll buy juice boxes and snacks like packaged raisins or granola bars.

2. Collect all your decorating supplies.

3. Decorate the lunch bags. Add shiny stickers or glitter so the bags look colorful. Draw or paint designs on every bag.

4. If you used paint on the bags, make sure to give it time to dry.

5. When the bags are ready, fill them. In each bag, put a granola bar, juice box, and a small toy that you got from a fast food restaurant. It's best not to add fresh fruit or sandwiches, because you don't know when the bags will be delivered to the kids. You don't want to end up giving them a smushed sandwich and a brown banana.

6. It might be fun to drop a small note into each bag. Just write something like "Hi. My name is Sara, and I'm in fifth grade. My dog's name is BoBo, and he snores. Hope you like the snack."

7. When the bags are full, fold the tops and hold the fold in place with a piece of tape.

8. Ask an adult to help you deliver the bags to a shelter. You probably won't get to see the kids at the shelter, but you can know they'll be happy for the snack and toy.

According to a "Future of Children" report, there are 68,000 homeless children in the US.

9. This is also a great project at a birthday party or for a Sunday school class. Ask different kids to bring granola bars or juice boxes. With a group of kids you can really put together a lot of Bedtime Snack Sacks.

Design Funky Umbrellas

You've probably heard people say, "It's raining cats and dogs." We know St. Bernards and Siamese kittens aren't really dropping from the sky. (That would hurt.) Incorporate that familiar saying into a fundraising activity to help cats and dogs at your local animal shelter. Perhaps you've been to a shelter and have seen all the abandoned animals in their pens. By raising money, you help the shelter afford to do more advertising to get animals adopted.

Here's What You'll Need

Plain, light-colored umbrellas (Try your local dollar or craft store.)

Decorating supplies such as waterproof paint, permanent markers, stencils, paintbrushes

Old newspaper

A popular store or business where you can set up a stand to sell the umbrellas

Supplies to set up your booth: table, chairs, cashbox, and posters or brochures about the animal shelter

A parent to help buy supplies and provide your transportation

Follow These Easy Steps

1. Ask the manager of a busy store or a business office if you can set up near their entrance to sell your customized umbrellas. Make sure to tell them where the money is going. Set a date for the Funky Umbrella sale.

2. Collect all your umbrellas and decorating supplies.

3. Ask a friend to help you decorate the umbrellas. Because umbrellas have panels, you could open the umbrella and set it down on a piece of newspaper for easy clean-up. Paint or color each panel one at a time, rotating the umbrella when it is time to decorate a new panel.

4. If you're going to use a stencil, tape the stencil onto the umbrella and spray paint around it. When you remove the stencil, you'll have a perfect outline.

5. On the day of the sale, set up your display table. It's great if you can sell the umbrellas on a rainy day. People will buy them to avoid getting wet.

6. Make sure people know how the proceeds will be used. Make posters or ask if you can borrow some from the animal shelter. Ask for brochures from the charity, too. Pass out the brochures to people so they can think about buying an umbrella while they shop or do business in the office building.

Many people think Seattle, Washington, is the rainiest city in the United States. Actually, Mobile, Alabama, wins that award. They get close to five feet of rain each year.

7. After you're done selling, take the money to the animal shelter. (Idea submitted by Reese Ravner.)

21 Celebrate "Stuffed with Hugs" Day

If your room is like mine, you have an assortment of stuffed animals ranging from cuddly aardvarks to striped zebras. But have you ever made a stuffed animal to be donated to a charity? Build-A-Bear Workshop stores are located in malls across the country and even overseas. These stores let you pick out the shell of a stuffed animal and then go to a special machine that blows stuffing into your animal. You insert a special fabric heart in the shell before adding the stuffing. You may have visited a Build-A-Bear Workshop to get a stuffed animal for yourself. Here's where the volunteering starts. Each year in May, on Stuffed with Hugs day, people are invited to visit any Build-A-Bear Workshop and make a bear for free. The bears are donated to a worthy cause. They've already distributed 215,000 teddy bears.

Here's What You'll Need

An adult to drive you to a Build-A-Bear Workshop store

Follow These Easy Steps

1. In early May look at the Build-A-Bear website (www.buildabear.com) and find the store closest to you.

2. Call the store for the exact date they will celebrate Stuffed with Hugs Day.

3. Have an adult take you to the store. She won't mind driving because she can make her own bear. Follow the directions from the friendly staff at the store about how to select and stuff your bear. Have a good time creating a special bear for a special person and donating it.

4. If you don't live close to a Build-A-Bear Workshop store, ask a friend or relative in a different community to participate.

Have you been involved in a major volunteer project? Why not apply to be a Huggable Hero? Build-A-Bear sponsors a yearly contest to honor twelve kids involved in volunteering. I was a winner for 2008. If you go to a Build-A-Bear Workshop store, ask for their free calendar. You'll see me on one of the pages.

5. Here's another way to volunteer through the Build-A-Bear Workshop. Are you involved with a church or nonprofit group? Ask the leader if they are a 501c3 organization. (They'll know what that means.) If they say yes, encourage them to apply for a Champ Grant through Build-A-Bear for a volunteer project. The grants range from $1,000 to $5,000, so your group could do an amazing project with the grant money. Have an adult contact giving@buildabear.com for all the details.

Get More Information

You'll find tons of games and activities on the Build-A-Bear Workshop website (www.buildabear.com).

Raise Funds with Dinosaur-Teeth Necklaces

22

Here's a unique item kids can make while earning money for a favorite charity. Actually, you don't have real dinosaur teeth, but dried carrot pieces look like a prehistoric item. It's fun making these necklaces because it's a different type of craft.

Here's What You'll Need

Carrots

Cutting board

Sharp knife

Embroidery floss

Needle with a large eye

Thin bamboo skewers (optional)

Assortment of pony beads (available at any craft store)

Table

Price signs

Change box

Follow These Easy Steps

1. Ask a parent to help you find a place to set up your dinosaur-necklace-making booth. The local park district or recreation department may have a list of upcoming events. Does your community have kids' road runs or concerts in the park? Call the event organizer and explain you'd like to set up a table where kids can make Dinosaur-Teeth Necklaces. Explain the money goes to a good cause.

2. Check with your local library. They might host a special dinosaur storytime where your craft table would be included as part of the program.

3. As soon as you have a location and date, get busy making dinosaur teeth. Ask a parent to help you cut the carrots into one-fourth- to one-half-inch slices.

4. Thread the large needle with embroidery floss and poke a hole in each carrot slice. If you wiggle the needle to make the hole bigger, it will help you in the future steps.

5. String the carrot slices onto the embroidery floss. Estimate you'll need about twelve to fifteen dried carrot slices (or dinosaur teeth) per necklace. If you have thin bamboo skewers, string the carrot slices over the skewers.

Ever wanted to own a real dinosaur tooth? www.paleoclones.com sells lifelike reproductions of dinosaur bones and teeth. You can even buy a velociraptor killing claw for $7.

6. The next step is to dry the carrot pieces. In the summer let them sit outside in the sun for two or three days. Indoors, put the carrot pieces near a heating vent or another warm, dry place. They'll shrivel and look very prehistoric.

7. Here's an important step: Once or twice a day, rotate the carrots on the floss or skewer so they don't stick.

8. Remove the prehistoric teeth and put them in a container for the day of the event.

9. When the big day arrives, set up a table, with a sign saying how much it costs to make a necklace. Have lengths of embroidery floss cut to eighteen inches. Let kids string the prehistoric teeth alternating with different colored pony beads. Tie the ends when the necklace is finished.

10. Thank the event organizers and donate all your hard-earned money.

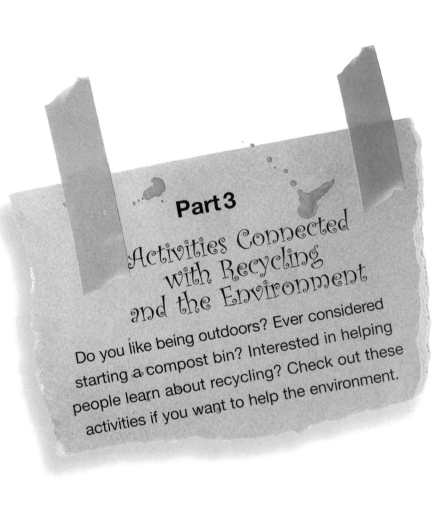

Part 3

Activities Connected with Recycling and the Environment

Do you like being outdoors? Ever considered starting a compost bin? Interested in helping people learn about recycling? Check out these activities if you want to help the environment.

Recycle with a Recycling Carnival

In 1970 the first Earth Day was celebrated on April 22. That day is designed to help improve the quality of our air, water, and living environment. While you can celebrate on the official Earth Day, volunteering related to environmental issues is possible all year round. Help people learn about the importance of recycling by sponsoring a recycling carnival.

Here's What You'll Need

Assortment of recyclable items like boxes, paper, cardboard, empty cans, empty plastic bottles

Paper for posters and flyers

Follow These Easy Steps

1. Find a place to hold your carnival. Check with your school or a community recreation center. If the weather is nice, you might plan to do the carnival outside in a parking lot or park.

2. This event needs volunteers to help you plan and run it. See if your dance class, scout troop, or church youth group can help. The more volunteers you have, the easier it will be for everyone.

3. Set a date, time, and location for the recycling carnival. Make posters and flyers to help publicize the event. Decide if you want the event to be free or to charge a small admission fee. Donate the money to a local recycling program.

4. Call other environment-related groups to see if they want to have information tables and pass out brochures about their programs.

5. Assign different people to set up carnival-type booths and activities. Try some of these ideas:

- Stack empty cans and have people try to knock them down with homemade beanbags made from unpopped popcorn poured into the toe of an old sock. (You'll want to tie a knot and cut off the excess sock.)
- Use empty plastic soda bottles for a recycled bowling game. People try to knock down the bottles with a ball.
- Use large cardboard refrigerator boxes to make castles or spaceships for kids to play in.
- Decorate cardboard boxes for a beanbag toss. Have an adult cut holes in the box so kids can try to throw a beanbag into the hole.
- Have a newspaper fashion show contest. Give groups of people stacks of old newspaper and masking tape. Allow a designated amount of time for each group to design a dress or outfit and have someone model the creation.

The average person in the US produces sixteen hundred pounds of trash a year. Seventy-five percent of that trash can be recycled.

6. When the carnival ends, make sure to recycle all the supplies you used.

Help Save the Rainforest

If you've ever watched educational programs on TV, you've seen how the rain forest is filled with exotic animals, leafy vines, and an amazing number of trees. Unfortunately, because more and more people need land to build houses and stores, the rainforest is being destroyed. When Janine Licare was nine-and-a-half, she wanted to help the rainforest in Costa Rica, where she lived. Since then, her organization, Kids Saving The Rain Forest, has bought four acres of land in the rainforest and started an animal rehabilitation center. They've planted more than five thousand trees and have sister schools in countries around the world. Janine's pledge is "We believe that the rainforest is a storehouse of treasures. We vow to do everything we can to save it. With the vanishing rainforest goes the future of our planet. We have to be the generation that makes a difference."

It just goes to show kids can change the world.

Follow These Easy Steps

1. Read books or look at websites about the rainforest. The more facts you have, the better you can inform people. Try these for starters:

Here's What You'll Need

Supplies vary, depending on your project.

www.therainforestsite.com
www.microsoft.com/kids/msbrainforest
www.amazonteam.org/kids
www.kidssavingtherainforest.org

2. If you have $50, sign up on "Save-an-Acre" (http://rainforest.org/help/save-an-acre.html). This program lets you "buy" an acre of rainforest and save it from destruction. You'll get a certificate saying you own one acre of rainforest.

3. Get your friends together and present a rainforest art show. Draw or paint pictures on recyclable paper that show animals and plants in the rainforest. Put the artwork on display so family and friends can buy the pictures. Contribute the money to an organization work-ing to save the rainforest.

The tropical rainforests cover just 2 percent of the earth's land surface, yet they are home to two-thirds of all the living species. A typical 4-mile-square patch of rainforest contains 1,500 species of flowering plants, 750 species of trees, 125 mammal species, 400 species of birds, 100 species of reptiles, 60 species of amphibians, and 150 different species of butterflies.

Get More Information

Read about Janine Licare's passion for saving the rain forest at her website (www.kidssavingtherainforest.org).

25   Plant a Tree

Just think what our world would look like if we didn't have any leafy trees. As more trees are cut down for paper, furniture, and houses, there's a need to raise awareness about the importance of trees. The National Arbor Day Foundation helps educate people around the country about planting and nurturing trees. Their website (www.arborday.org) gives you plenty of ideas on how to encourage your family and friends to plant trees and do what they can to reduce waste so more trees don't have to be cut down.

Here's What You'll Need

$10 (your money will go a long way with this project)

Assorted supplies

Follow These Easy Steps

1. One of the easiest ways to help the environment is to plant trees. Don't worry. You don't have to dig a huge hole and drag a twenty-foot tree into your backyard. Join the National Arbor Day Foundation for $10. In addition to getting a membership card, they'll send you ten trees that grow in your specific area. The foundation sends the trees when it's the best time to plant in your community. Obviously December isn't a good time to plant trees in Northern Minnesota, but if you live in Florida, that's a different story.

2. You can plan an Arbor Day celebration. Here's an interesting fact about Arbor Day:

Each state celebrates on a different day. So check out their website and see when to plan your activity to celebrate Arbor Day. Maybe you could help a local park plant trees. How about asking a senior center if they'd like you to plant a few trees? Encourage other people to join the Arbor Day Foundation so they'll get ten free trees to plant. Have a block party with games and refreshments, passing out flyers about the importance of trees. Enjoy a picnic in the shade of a giant tree.

3. Learn about trees any time of year on the National Arbor Day Foundation website (www.arborday.org). There you'll find fun activities like tree identification pictures, games, puzzles, and information on how to join the Nature Explorer Club, Home Edition.

4. If you are in fifth grade, enter the National Poster Contest, and you could win some fun prizes.

When you think of trees, you probably picture their trunks as being round. A few miles north of the Panama Canal Zone is the "valley of square trees." This is the only known place in the world where trees have rectangular trunks.

Get More Information

Contact the National Arbor Day Foundation (www.arborday.org) to learn more about the importance of planting trees.

Help the Environment the Easy Way

Yes, it's great to think about reducing global warming or ending world hunger. But how do you start working on a problem that stumps scientists and experts? Sometimes, a good way to volunteer is by joining an established program. That's the benefit of working with a group such as Kids F.A.C.E. This kids' environmental group is set up to help you start a chapter in your community.

Here's What You'll Need

Supplies vary, depending on your project.

Follow These Easy Steps

1. Kids F.A.C.E. stands for Kids **for a C**lean Environment.

2. Go on their website (www.kidsface.org) to enroll your chapter. They'll send you membership packets, certificates, ideas for group projects, and brochures.

3. Plan an introductory meeting and invite your friends. Have an adult help you find a location and time where you can meet. Send out e-mails or flyers, letting people know how they can be a part of a group helping the environment.

4. Make your first meeting interesting. Explain how Kids F.A.C.E. is an organized program with activities encouraging people to recycle, plant trees and shrubs, and raise awareness of the environment. They focus on finding solutions instead of putting blame on others. If possible, suggest two or three projects and have the group vote on which they like best. That way the group is involved in working on an activity right away.

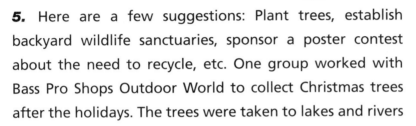

5. Here are a few suggestions: Plant trees, establish backyard wildlife sanctuaries, sponsor a poster contest about the need to recycle, etc. One group worked with Bass Pro Shops Outdoor World to collect Christmas trees after the holidays. The trees were taken to lakes and rivers and sunk to the bottom. Now they give a nesting place for fish to lay their eggs.

6. The staff at Kids F.A.C.E. is available if you have questions or need ideas. Call them at 800-952-3223.

You might like having an endangered animal ringtone on your cell phone. Click on www.rareearthtones.org and the site will send you the sound of a whooping crane or beluga whale.

Get More Information

The Kids F.A.C.E. website (www.kidsface.org) has lots more information about getting involved. Check them out!

Build a Rock Garden

Do you know a senior or someone who enjoys being outdoors but can't maintain a fancy garden? Brighten that person's life by building him or her a small rock garden. An advantage to rock gardens is they are easy to maintain, yet still add color and interest to an ordinary area. The cost is low, yet the enjoyment factor is high.

Here's What You'll Need

A variety of rocks—You might find some in your own yard or by a river. Rocks are available at a low cost at home improvement stores or landscape centers. In most cases, neighbors or relatives have rocks around their yards they'd be glad to donate.

Soil

Assorted plants that grow well around rocks

Shovel and rake

Access to water

Follow These Easy Steps

1. Select a location that can be easily viewed. You don't need a large space, since this rock garden is designed to serve as a place for a senior to enjoy being outdoors and enjoy nature. An area around four feet by four feet is a good start. You can always make it bigger.

2. Use the rake to prepare your area. Be creative in how you set up the rock garden. Make mounds of dirt and place rocks around the edges. Decide if you want to put more rocks around the edges. Use the dirt to fill in any space around the rocks. Add water to moisten the dirt.

3. Now you are ready to plant. Use plants that like a rocky environment. Try these: phlox, crocus, veronica, alyssum, and sedum. (Funny names, but they grow well in rock gardens.)

4. If you live in a warm climate, try planting a few cacti. (We live in Seattle, so a cactus would never grow in my rock garden.)

5. Use additional dirt to put around the plants. Pat the dirt firmly to remove air bubbles in the hole.

6. Rearrange the rocks if you need to. Remember plants will start to grow over and around the rocks.

7. Give your rock garden another spray of water to make the plants happy.

8. Place a chair nearby so people can sit and enjoy your creation.

For inspiration, look at the Stonesmith website (http://www.stonesmith.net/RG.html) to see examples of amazing rock gardens.

Recycle at Home

Some volunteer projects require hours of work and involve lots of people. Have you ever considered that you can do a simple volunteer project in your own home? Encourage your family to try to reduce the amount of trash they produce. Even one family's effort makes a difference. You've probably heard the phrase "reduce, reuse, recycle." These three words can help your family be green environmentally.

Here's What You'll Need

Plastic recycling bins

Canvas grocery bags

Reusable food containers

Follow These Easy Steps

1. Have a family meeting to talk about ways to recycle. Let them know that the average family generates 4.3 pounds of trash a day. Your family's goal is to reduce that amount. That's one time it's good to be below average.

2. Make a list of suggestions, so people can see ways to reduce the trash they produce. Here are a few to get you started:

- Ask your parents to buy items in bulk, rather than individual packages. Buy one big container of juice instead of individual juice boxes. Large boxes of cereal have less packaging than single-sized boxes.

- Use reusable containers for your lunch instead of plastic bags and juice boxes.
- Use canvas bags instead of paper or plastic bags when buying groceries, since the cloth bag can be used over and over.

Here's a startling statistic: The United States has only 6 percent of the world's population, yet we produce over half the world's garbage.

- If possible, buy CDs, books, and other items at garage sales or thrift stores. You save money while reducing the amount of plastic and paper used in buying new items.
- Keep track of how many garbage bags your family fills in one week. Try to reduce that number.
- Recycle old batteries. Many drugstores have containers for old batteries, which are disposed of properly.
- This might be tough, but try to cut back on fast-food meals. You'll be saving on all those Styrofoam containers.
- Instead of throwing out old furniture or clothes, donate items to Goodwill or Salvation Army. Your donation reduces waste and provides bargains for other people.
- Find out where the closest recycling center is in your community. They often provide containers so you can sort and recycle paper, glass, plastic, etc.

Get a Passport in Time

Do you enjoy reading about history? Ever wish you could search for dinosaur bones? Passport in Time (sponsored by the USDA Forest Service) offers you unique volunteer opportunities. These activities do require you have an adult with you, but maybe you can convince the family to make a vacation out of a Passport in Time experience. You'll work alongside professional forest service archeologists and historians on national forests throughout the US. You'll choose from archeological digs, rock art restoration, oral history gathering, and analysis of artifacts. Groups have excavated a nineteenth-century Chinese mining site and restored a lookout tower in Oregon.

Here's What You'll Need

Passport in Time staff provide all the equipment you need for your project. You just need to bring comfortable and safe work clothes. A list of items needed will be sent after you and an adult register.

Follow These Easy Steps

1. Convince an adult to participate in one of these activities. The program is free, but you need to get to the location. In some cases you'll need to bring your own camping equipment and food. Some volunteers stay in local hotels. If your family has an RV, you often can bring it close to the site.

2. After you have a willing adult, find a program. Volunteer projects fill up fast, so sign up as soon as possible.

3. Be prepared to work alongside professional archeologists and historians. You'll be contributing to important issues dealing with the environment and historical research. Don't worry, there's plenty of time for fun and relaxation.

4. Keep track of your Passport in Time passport, a book that records all your volunteer activities. Every time you visit a project, the project leader stamps your passport and records your hours worked. It makes a great souvenir from this volunteer experience.

If you like digging, you'll probably find rocks with unusual shapes and designs. Check out the weird rocks at Nature Made Rocks (www.naturemaderocks.com). You'll see rocks that have "pictures" on them like Fred Flintstone or a scared dog.

Get More Information

Check out the Passport in Time website at www.passportintime.com for a list of upcoming projects.

Reduce, Reuse, Recycle

Think about all the paper items in your school classroom. There's paper on the bulletin board, decorations, posters, books, and lots of writing paper. Paper is everywhere. Sometimes we write a few words on a piece of paper and throw it away. Start a recycling program at your school and get everyone to reduce, reuse, recycle.

Here's What You'll Need

Cardboard boxes

Markers, crayons, and paper (recycled, of course) to decorate the boxes

Follow These Easy Steps

1. Talk to your teachers about your idea to start this project. Some schools have recycling programs in place, but often few people know about them.

2. Have an adult help you call a recycling center or government agency in your community. They often have school assembly programs where professionals give interesting presentations about recycling. You might even get a visit from Recycler Ricky, the Recycling Raccoon.

3. Start out small. Have a contest to decorate paper recycling boxes. Then place the boxes next to the wastebasket in each classroom. Make sure each box is clearly labeled "paper recycling." Encourage classmates to put unwanted papers into the cute boxes instead of the wastebasket.

4. Look for ways to reduce the use of paper. Can you write on both sides? What about using scraps of construction paper for craft projects?

5. Don't forget the teacher's lounge. Place recycling boxes next to the staff wastebasket and the copy machine.

6. Be sure to have a way to get the classroom boxes of recycled paper picked up. Your city sanitation department might give you dumpsters to collect all those pieces of paper.

7. Many schools have to pay according to the weight of their trash. When you throw away half-full cartons of milk or juice boxes, it adds to the cost. Get students to remember "drink, drain, drop." This means you first "drink" as much of the milk or juice as possible. Then "drain" the leftover liquid into a sink. Finally, "drop" the container in the trash. Now your trash doesn't weigh as much.

8. As interest in recycling grows, expand to collecting cans and plastic bottles. You could even start a compost pile from leftover cafeteria food.

Don't forget to recycle the phone books at your school. Phone books are already made of about 40 percent recycled materials.

Get More Information

Take a look at www.epa.gov/recyclecity for fun games and activities all about recycling.

Be a Junior Forest Ranger

31

Do you like nature and animals? The USDA Forest Service (those are the people who greet you at national campgrounds and monuments) has a program for seven- to thirteen-year-olds called the Junior Forest Rangers. What's great about this program is you can do it in your own community. You don't have to travel hundreds of miles to reach the wilderness, yet you'll still learn about fire safety and conserving natural resources.

Here's What You'll Need

Supplies vary, depending on the project.

Follow These Easy Steps

1. Go on the USDA Forest Service website to get the Junior Forest Ranger Adventure Guide. This gives you all the information you need to complete the program and help the environment.

2. Ask an adult to help you complete the activities in the Adventure Guide.

3. After finishing the guide, send the Junior Forest Ranger form to the address on the back page.

4. You'll get an embroidered badge, a pin, an oath card, and a Junior Forest Ranger card. The card is handy because it has an ID number that lets you get on the Junior

Forest Ranger website. This site offers games and activities to help you learn more about our forests and conservation.

5. Along with completing the Junior Forest Ranger program, you can get involved with Woodsy Owl. You've probably seen this owl on commercials, saying, "Give a hoot; don't pollute." The USDA will send someone to your school dressed as Woodsy Owl to teach kids about the importance of not polluting. Wouldn't it be fun to walk through the school halls with Woodsy Owl? Contact your local USDA Forest Service Office to set a time for Woodsy Owl to come to a school assembly. Coordinate with your school principal about the best day and time.

A popular character sponsored by the USDA Forest Service is Smokey Bear. He gets so much mail, he has his own zip code.

Get More Information

Find out more about the Junior Forest Ranger guide at the WSDA Forest Service website (www.fs.fed.us/spf/com). There is a link that says "Information by State." Click on your state for local information.

Pick Up Parks

Isn't it wonderful to walk through a park and see trees, animals, and even different types of moss? However, it isn't nice to see garbage and trash on the side of a trail. Cleaning a park or beach is a great way to keep nature beautiful. You may be reading this and thinking, *I don't even like cleaning my room; why would I want to clean something as big as a park?* If you'll get a group of your friends to work with you, you'll be surprised at how much fun you can have while helping the environment.

Here's What You'll Need

Garbage bags

Garden or work gloves

Follow These Easy Steps

1. Have an adult help you call the local parks and recreation office. Let them know you would like to be involved in helping clean a park or rebuilding a trail. Most parks departments have ongoing programs that need volunteers. Our parks department had volunteers widening trails. It was fun because they used donkeys to help pull large logs out of the trails. The staff at the parks department will give you details for an organized clean-up project or suggest something for you to do on your own.

2. Get friends to help on the clean-up day. It's always more fun to work on a project with friends. If this is a park-sponsored event, they'll probably supply rakes or gloves. In addition to helping spruce up the park, you'll see how inconsiderate people can be as you pick up discarded soda cans and gum wrappers. My sister did a park clean-up and found eight dirty diapers along the trail.

3. If you are doing a clean-up project on your own, make sure an adult is with you. While parks are generally safe, you don't want to be by yourself on a deserted park trail, miles from other people. For individual projects, you could plant trees, put down trail markers, paint birdhouses, or pick up trash.

The largest national park in the United States is Wrangell St. Elias National Park in Alaska. The park is bigger than New Hampshire and Vermont combined.

Get More Information

The National Recreation and Park Association website (www.nrpa.org) lists state parks and recreation contacts. You're sure to find someone who can help you with your desire to clean up the environment.

Part 4

An Assortment of Tasks to Try

Still not sure what kind of volunteer project to try? Check out these general volunteering activities.

Put Together a Christmas Gift Bag

33

Last Christmas you probably had a pile of presents under the tree and a stocking stuffed with candy and toys. Can you imagine what it would be like to have a Christmas without presents? Children who suffer because of war, disease, poverty, or natural disasters may never know the delight of opening a gift. You can change that.

Here's What You'll Need

Gallon-size plastic zipper bag

Assortment of school supplies, hard candies, socks, or trinkets

A picture of yourself and a short letter

$5 to help pay for shipping each bag

Permanent markers

Follow These Easy Steps

1. Decorate the gallon-size plastic bag with permanent markers to give the bag a festive look.

2. Check out the World Hope website under "Children's Gift Paks" (http://www.worldhope.org/hopeforchildren/giftpak.htm). You'll find a list of categories to choose from. You might decide to fill the bag for a young child or designate the bag as a "school kit."

3. After you've decided on an age group, start collecting items to put in the bag. Fill the bag with the items suggested on the website. Just remember, don't send any war-type toys, chocolate, or anything liquid.

4. Be sure to label the bag with the age of the child, and if it is for a boy or girl. Labels can be printed from the website, or you can create your own label and fasten it to the bag.

5. It's a fun idea to include a picture of yourself and a short note to the child who will receive your gift. For your security, *do not include your address*.

6. Include $5 per bag to help cover shipping. Place a check or cash in an envelope and tape (don't staple) it to the outside of the gift pak. Make checks payable to World Hope International, Inc.

7. Have an adult help you ship the bag to

World Hope Warehouse
1906 Gus Kaplan Dr.
Alexandria, LA 71301

or check the website for a drop-off location near you.

Christmas Gift Paks are hand delivered to children in developing countries through World Hope International and partnering organizations. So far, they've given out more than 15,000 gift paks. For some children, it's the first present they've ever received.

Get More Information

 Check out the website at www.worldhope.org or contact the organization at 888-466-4673.

34

Give a GospelShoe

Looking for a clever way to volunteer and also share the gospel story? You probably have seen the wordless book or made a wordless bracelet. Now you can buy a "wordless shoe" or GospelShoe. Each color represents a part of the story about our salvation. The black on the shoe represents our sin, while the red reminds us that Christ died to cover our sins. The green section of the shoe reminds us to grow with God.

Here's What You'll Need

Simply register with www.gospelshoe.org and they'll send you any supplies you need

Follow These Easy Steps

1. Talk to your pastor or youth group leader if you can give a short speech about the GospelShoe program.

2. If he or she agrees, prepare your presentation.

3. Are you trying to raise money for a youth group camping trip or special event? One idea is to ask the adults in your church to buy a GospelShoe as a special fundraiser. You will "sell" them the shoes, plus an additional amount that goes to your fund raising event. For example: sell two pairs of GospelShoe flip flops for $10.00. Six dollars will go to GospelShoe and $4.00 will go to your fundraising event. Your church members can donate the shoes to mission projects, or GospelShoe will see that the shoes go to deserving people.

4. You could also simply ask the congregation for a special offering. With the money, purchase a GospelShoe and give them to people in need. By giving people these shoes, you are sharing the Good News while also meeting a basic need in someone's life. Many churches buy a GospelShoe and then send them to their church supported orphanages or schools overseas. Those overseas pastors use the colors on the shoes as a way to explain the gospel to people who don't have a Bible.

5. Simply register on the GospelShoe website and they'll give you all sorts of help such as: a DVD with 1-, 2-, and 4-minute promos and testimonies, posters to place around your church, PowerPoint slides, bulletin inserts and postcards, GospelShoe offering envelopes, sample shoes to put on display, and GospelShoe prayer bracelets for your church members.

> You probably simply go to a store and buy shoes when you need a pair. Matthew McGrory was born in 1973. He grew to be over seven feet tall and wore size 29 shoes! They had to be custom made and cost thousands of dollars.

Get More Information

You can see the two types of these fun shoes on their website at www.gospelshoe.org.

Promote
Senior Computer Skills

What do you do when you need to find the capital of Peru? How do you find out how to build a doghouse? You get on the computer and look for the information. Kids our age take the computer for granted. But what about grandparents? Are they comfortable on the computer? Here's a way to volunteer to help a senior citizen use e-mail and maybe even surf the Net.

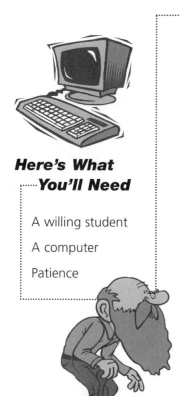

Here's What You'll Need

A willing student

A computer

Patience

Follow These Easy Steps

1. Think about elderly people you know who might want to learn how to use the computer. Call a local senior center to see if they have seniors looking to become familiar with a computer. Assisted living centers have active seniors eager to increase their skills.

2. I just read a notice in our newspaper that the senior center has eight new computers, but needs instructors.

3. After you have a student, talk to him (or her) about his goals. Does he want to learn how to e-mail his grandkids? I met a lady who just wanted to look up recipes. If you know the senior's interest, you'll have a better idea what to teach.

4. Begin your first lesson by saying, "Show me what you know about the computer." That way you'll see if you need to start with the basics of logging on or if you can be more advanced and teach how to send pictures with e-mail.

5. Be flexible and patient. Seniors grew up using typewriters but might feel intimidated by a computer. Let them know everyone makes mistakes at first. (Did you ever accidentally delete a report just as you wanted to print it out?) Allow time for your student to ask questions.

6. Let your student have as much hands-on experience as possible. It's tempting for you to move the mouse all around and say, "Just click on Insert, then go to page number, then . . . ," but watching you move the mouse won't help your student learn the process. He needs to get used to moving the mouse and getting the curser to go in the right place.

7. Encourage your student to write down notes. You'll be giving him lots of information, and notes help him remember your tips.

8. Most seniors need three or four lessons to feel comfortable on the computer. Offer to meet with them in a week, after they've practiced the skills you've taught them. They may surprise you by e-mailing you a thank-you note.

In fifth grade, our class had seniors come every Wednesday afternoon and we'd teach them computer skills. One woman picked up the mouse and pointed it at the computer. She thought she was supposed to use the mouse the same way as a remote control.

36 Use Pen-and-Paper Power

Have you ever been frustrated by something happening in your community, but didn't know what to do about it? When I was twelve, our city spent over $1 million building a simple walking bridge across a busy street. I thought that was too expensive and a waste of money, so I wrote to the mayor. Sometimes sending letters to local and national leaders can make a difference. My mom heard about a company that does painful research on dogs to test hair care products. She wrote them, saying she wouldn't buy their products if they kept up the testing by putting shampoo in the dogs' eyes. The president wrote her back and told her they were looking into other research possibilities.

Write a letter and have your opinion heard.

Here's What You'll Need

Paper and pens

Stamps

Envelopes

Addresses

Follow These Easy Steps

1. What are you passionate about? What gets you fired up? Are you upset because your dog has to be on a leash at the park? Has a story on the news pulled at your heartstrings? Do your homework. Know what you are talking about. Go online and research the topic if it's controversial. Maybe the dog leash law was put into place because a dog bit a child. Present your position with a strong point. Back up your point with statistics and facts.

2. Don't forget to write positive letters. Did you go to a store and get great service? Write a letter to the manager, telling her about your experience. If your family goes out to eat and the waiter is extra friendly, take time to write a letter to the restaurant. You'll make both the restaurant manager and the waiter happy.

3. When you write, use a computer or your best handwriting. Keep the letter short and to the point. Be sure to ask for a response. Maybe you are writing the mayor because the city government has closed a community center due to budget cuts. Explain how you and your friends enjoyed going to the center. Ask the mayor to reconsider his or her budget.

4. Always include your name and address on both the envelope and letter so you can get a reply.

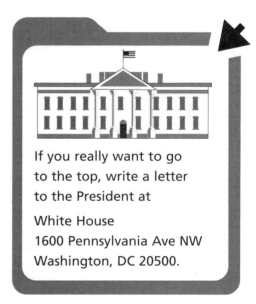

If you really want to go to the top, write a letter to the President at

White House
1600 Pennsylvania Ave NW
Washington, DC 20500.

Get More Information

Look on http://www.usa.gov/index.shtml or www.congresslink.org/print to find the addresses of government leaders.

Organize a Scrubbing Extravaganza

If you attend church regularly, you probably don't even notice the vacuumed carpet and clean sidewalks. You take it for granted that the youth group room is set up for your wild activities. Some churches have paid custodians, while others use volunteers to keep everything clean. Either way, show your appreciation for your pastor or youth group leader by sprucing up your church or youth group room. The regular church custodian probably does routine cleaning to keep the church looking good. This is your chance to do the extras that normally don't get done.

Here's What You'll Need

Vacuum cleaners

Buckets

Cleaners

Rags

Trash bags

Friends to help

Follow These Easy Steps

1. Talk to your pastor or youth group leader about your plans to have a cleaning extravaganza to get the church looking extra clean. See if they have specific tasks to do. Maybe they'd like the stained sofas in the choir room shampooed or want the curtains in the nursery washed. Did you play a crazy game and put marks on the wall during your last youth group meeting? You might find yourself washing those walls.

2. Figure out a time when you and your friends can get together to work. Pick a day when you won't disrupt an event going on

at that time. The choir won't appreciate your vacuuming as they rehearse for the Easter musical.

3. Make sure the church is unlocked. One group of teens planned to clean the sanctuary on a Saturday morning but couldn't get into the church. It's also good to let the church office know when you arrive so they don't think crazy teenagers are just hanging out.

4. Get a mom or two to help. They'll give tips on cleaning. You wouldn't want to pour straight bleach on a carpet stain.

Some people don't like to pollute the air with harsh cleaning chemicals. They use baking soda to scrub sinks and toilets. Try it.

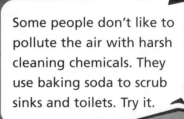

5. If no one else is around, bring a boom box and play music to make cleaning more fun.

6. If you have plants or grassy areas around the church, pick up any garbage that's scattered around. Take clippers and trim the bushes or plants outside the church.

7. Pack up your cleaning supplies and enjoy a super-clean church.

Volunteer with a Unique Camp

38

Do you have fun memories of going to camp run by crazy counselors playing wacky games? Your mom or dad probably kissed you good-bye and told you how much they'd miss you. But not all kids come from loving homes. While we don't like to think about it, there are thousands of children who come from abusive homes. Their parents might yell or even hit them. Royal Family Kids' Camps across the country serve battered, broken, and neglected children. Their goal is to provide positive memories in a Christian setting for kids who don't have many positive memories. While kids your age are too young to volunteer to work at the camp, you can help in other ways.

Here's What You'll Need

Supplies vary, depending on the project.

Follow These Easy Steps

1. Royal Family Kids' Camps run programs just like any other camp. Kids swim, make arts and crafts projects, sleep in cabins, and play games. However, since many of the campers don't have loving adults in their lives, the camp looks for volunteer "aunts and uncles" to spend time with the campers. These aunts and uncles go on walks with kids and spend one-to-one time together. This helps kids learn adult people care about them. You can help by finding adults who would volunteer a week at camp to be an aunt or uncle. Let a teacher or 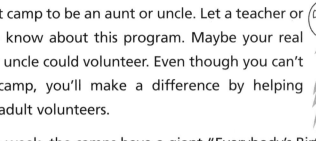 relative know about this program. Maybe your real aunt or uncle could volunteer. Even though you can't be at camp, you'll make a difference by helping recruit adult volunteers.

2. Each week, the camps have a giant "Everybody's Birthday Party." Many of these kids don't have the chance to celebrate their birthdays at home. At camp, everyone's birthday gets recognized with cakes, balloons, and presents. You can help by collecting party decorations and supplies. Donate candles, streamers, and balloons to make the party extra festive.

3. Here's a unique way to volunteer. Many of the campers are scared of the dark. For $6 you can buy a Royal Family Kids' Camps nightlight. Campers use the nightlights at camp and take them home as a reminder of their safe time at camp.

Looking for a really unusual camp to attend this summer? If you are a teenager, you can go to the Summer Explosive Camp sponsored by the University of Missiouri-Rolla Engineering School. You learn to use explosives and actually help blow up 20,000 tons of rock!

Get More Information

 Contact the staff of Royal Family Kids' Camp (www.rfkc.org) to find specific ways you can volunteer.

Help Special Athletes

You've probably heard people talking about Special Olympics, but you may not be quite sure what it is. Well, Special Olympics is a worldwide organization that helps people with intellectual disabilities to become physically fit, productive, and respected members of society through sports. They offer thirty Olympic-type summer and winter sports ranging from bowling to gymnastics to swimming, and 2.5 million Special Olympic athletes compete. It takes more than 700,000 volunteers to make the program a success. There are many ways for you to participate.

Here's What You'll Need

Comfortable clothes and shoes

Follow These Easy Steps

1. Because Special Olympics serve people in more than 165 countries, there's sure to be a local program close to you. Check out the Special Olympics website to find a contact person in your community.

2. Ask if you can observe one of their practices. Sometimes it's uncomfortable being around someone in a wheelchair or with a speech impediment. Observe for a while, and soon you'll see the athletes have personalities just like you and your friends. You may end up making new friends from Special Olympic athletes.

3. A volunteer coordinator will probably explain jobs you can do. You'll have a short training orientation to help you feel comfortable with what you'll be doing. I once helped a Special Olympics athlete learn how to stay in her lane while running the 100-meter dash. Other possibilities might be timekeeper, scorekeeper, or athlete escort to get the athletes where they need to be at the right time.

4. Sometimes Special Olympics athletes compete in regional and state competitions. There you might volunteer to help sell concessions or make families feel welcome. Perhaps you'll greet athletes when they arrive or be in charge of clean-up. The point is, Special Olympics offers a wide variety of ways to volunteer.

If you plan to volunteer with Special Olympics, you should know the oath all athletes recite: "Let me win, but if I cannot win, let me be brave in the attempt."

Get More Information

 The Special Olympics website (www.specialolympics.org) gives you all the information you need to get involved.

40

Clean Baby Drool

Who can resist a chubby, adorable baby with a big toothless smile? It's so much fun to play with babies, even if all they do is laugh as you put a box over your head. Maybe you already volunteer in the church nursery so parents can listen to the sermon without being distracted by a squirmy baby. But babies do put almost everything they touch into their mouths. This causes all the rattles, balls, and toys in the nursery to get covered with baby drool. This means it's easy for germs to spread as babies play. You can help keep babies healthy by volunteering to clean and disinfect the nursery toys. This is one of those behind-the-scenes volunteer jobs that needs to be done, but no one is excited about doing it. Maybe you can make this a family project where you all volunteer together after the service.

Follow These Easy Steps

Here's What You'll Need

Warm water

Rags or paper towels

Bleach or other disinfectant

(The church nursery probably has all these supplies.)

1. Talk to the person in charge of the church nursery. Explain how you'd like to volunteer for the unglamorous job of disinfecting baby toys. The director will be happy to have help. After being around babies all morning, he or she will appreciate having one less chore to do.

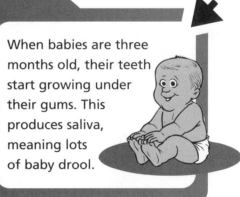

2. Follow the procedure the church has for disinfecting toys. Usually this means filling a tub or sink with warm water, soap, and disinfectant. Place the plastic toys in the water, wash, and rinse. Letting the toys air dry reduces the chance of germs being spread from a drying towel.

3. Dip a paper towel in the disinfectant water and wipe down door knobs, handles on rocking horses, and other items too big to fit in your tub of soapy water.

4. Now the babies have clean toys to play with—until they pick up an item and drool all over it again. At least you know this is one volunteer project that will never end.

When babies are three months old, their teeth start growing under their gums. This produces saliva, meaning lots of baby drool.

41

Give Back
to the Givers

You've been getting all kinds of ideas about volunteer projects from this book. Have you ever thought one way to volunteer is to honor volunteers? Often people work behind the scenes and don't get the thanks they deserve. Here's a way for you to volunteer by volunteering to help volunteers.

Here's What You'll Need

Supplies vary, depending on your project.

Follow These Easy Steps

1. Find a group of volunteers you want to acknowledge. How about planning something special for all the children's workers at your church, all the scout leaders in your community, or the volunteer coaches in your ball league?

2. After you have a designated volunteer group, figure out ways to honor all their volunteer efforts. Here are some ideas:

- Get a large piece of poster board and make a big thank-you card. Get lots of people to sign it and write personal comments. For example, if your card is for a soccer coach, get the team members to sign the card.
- Decorate a bulletin board with a sign that says something like "We Appreciate Our Children's Church Workers." Add

colorful borders and pictures.

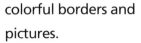

- Put together small "We Thank You" gift baskets filled with items relating to your group. Girl Scout leaders would appreciate baskets with sweet-smelling soaps, candles, cute note pads, and chocolate.

You might meet some great kid volunteers. Why not nominate them on the Amazing Kids website (www.amazingkids.com)? Each month an amazing kid is highlighted. Check out the website and be inspired by kids your own age.

- If all the volunteers are in one place, have selected people give each volunteer a flower, along with an explanation of why the volunteer is appreciated.

- Food is always appreciated. If you are honoring the greeters at your church, set up a table with special treats and a sign saying, "Thank you for having a sweet smile on your face when people arrive at church. Here are some sweets for you."

- Ask people to write individual thank-you notes. One church passed out paper and pencils during the Sunday service so everyone could write a note of appreciation to a woman who volunteered as a choir director for ten years. It thrilled her to read all the nice things people said about her.

  - If the group has a newsletter, talk to the editor about having a regular "Meet Our Volunteer" column. Each issue could include information and recognition about a different volunteer.

42

Buy a "Kid"

Childcare Worldwide is an organization that's special to me. Since 2002, I've been volunteering with them as they help children in developing countries get an education and break the cycle of poverty. I've seen their programs in Kenya, Uganda, and Mexico. In Lima, Peru, Childcare feeds breakfast to 11,500 kids every morning. Childcare offers group homes for children without parents. In the group home, kids get nutritious meals, Bible lessons, and a chance to go to school.

You can be sure any money you send will go to good use. Ninety-six percent of Childcare's budget goes directly to help children get medical attention, mosquito nets, books, and school uniforms. Pick one of the following ways to volunteer with Childcare Worldwide.

Here's What You'll Need

Supplies vary, depending on the project.

Follow These Easy Steps

1. How about participating in the Kids for Kids program? You, as a kid can buy a "kid," a baby goat, for a child in Africa. For $25, a staff member in Africa selects a needy child and buys him or her a goat. The child learns how to take care of the goat so it stays healthy. The family enjoys fresh goat milk and eventually that goat, along with others in the village, produces a small herd of goats. Families sell extra goat milk and earn money to live a better life.

2. You also could buy a Survival Pak to fight malnutrition. In many parts of the world, children have little chance of getting nutritious food. Many children show signs of malnutrition by an unnaturally extended belly. A $30 Survival Pak is a food package filled with nutritious basics like rice, beans, lentils, cooking oil, and flour. Childcare staff find families who desperately need food and give them Survival Paks.

3. Perhaps your family could sponsor a child overseas. For $35 a month, your family is matched with a child in Africa, Thailand, India, or Haiti. Your sponsorship pays that child's tuition, uniforms, books, medical care, and gives him or her a chance to attend church or Sunday school. You get pictures of your child and can write letters back. I've been sponsoring a girl named Annette for six years. We met when I was in Africa. I love exchanging letters and pictures with her. Thirty-five dollars a month is probably too expensive for you to do on your own, so you'll need your parents' help. I met a family who decided to give up cable TV and use the money to sponsor a child instead. Go to Childcare's website to see photos of kids looking for sponsors.

I sent some Frisbees to the children I met in Africa through Childcare Worldwide. They had never seen Frisbees and put them on their heads like flat hats!

Get More Information

 Childcare's website (www.childcareworldwide.org) has all the information you need.

Wear Jeans for a Cause

43

Does your school have a strict dress code? Maybe a semi-strict dress code? Many schools require uniforms or have guidelines against wearing jeans or hats. This idea is a great way to raise money for a good cause while allowing kids to wear something outside the dress code. It's a simple idea. Students pay a certain amount of money to be allowed to wear a "forbidden" clothing item. In my school (with a strict dress code), we'd occasionally get the chance to pay $2 to wear jeans for the day. With almost a thousand students, we'd raise nearly $2,000 in one single day.

Here's What You'll Need

Poster board to make signs

Markers or paint to make the signs

Flyers (optional)

Money collection envelopes (can be brown lunch bags)

Follow These Easy Steps

1. Go to the principal of your school and present the idea. Make sure to tell him where the money will be going and what it will do to help the world. Let him know kids can change the world, even by wearing hats to school.

2. Pick an item to wear. If kids at your school normally wear uniforms, just wearing regular clothes is a treat they'd be willing to pay $2 for. Maybe charge $1 to wear a hat or jeans.

3. Set a day for the event.

4. Pick a cause. Choose an organization or project where you want the money to go.

5. In most cases, parents give their children the money to wear the clothing item. Prepare flyers describing the charity. This makes parents feel good about donating money.

6. Put up signs around school telling people about the fund-raiser. Ask if you can give a short commercial during morning school announcements.

7. Tell teachers they can participate if they pay double the student fee.

8. On the day of the fund-raiser, give large envelopes to all the homeroom teachers. Have them collect the money from the students wearing the designated clothing item. At the end of the day, collect the envelopes from all the teachers. Make sure to count the money so you can tell your school how much you raised and how much everyone helped.

Do your parents say designer jeans are too expensive? Tell them APO Jeans offers jeans with diamond buttons and rivets that cost $4,000.

9. Have an adult write one check for the total amount and donate it to the charity of your choice.

Put On a Show

44

Do you love acting, singing, dancing, or playing an instrument? Do you have unusual talents you love to share with others? Get a group of your friends together and put on a talent show for a local senior center. Many seniors don't get a chance to leave the center and would love seeing youth perform. Don't worry if you hit the wrong note or drop your baton while twirling. The residents will love watching your energy and enthusiasm. So put your talents to good use and put on a great show for a great audience.

Here's What You'll Need

Your talents

Props for the acts

Costumes

Posters

Follow These Easy Steps

1. Contact a senior center or assisted-living facility. You can usually get contacts by looking in the yellow pages under Senior Services. Ask to speak to the activities director or volunteer coordinator. Explain what you want to do. They'll give you details about the best time and format.

2. Offer to make posters for the volunteer coordinator to put around the building. That way more people will attend.

3. Get a group of your friends who like to perform. Make sure you have a variety of talents. Is someone a great violinist? Can someone do magic? Is there a group of girls who can do a dance together? Try to get unusual talents, too. Can someone demonstrate how to train a dog? Does a friend know how to yodel?

4. Make sure everyone is prepared and ready to perform. If possible, have a dress rehearsal ahead of time. See if anyone needs special equipment. Is someone going to play the piano? Call ahead and make sure there is a piano where you will be performing. As the "director" of this talent show, plan the order of the acts. Start with a "splashy" first act and save the biggest and best act for last. Prepare an introduction for each act.

5. Call the senior center the day ahead of the show to confirm you are coming.

6. On the day of the performance, arrive early to make sure the room is ready. Once you have everything in place and the audience is seated, it's on with the show.

I love Broadway musicals. *The Phantom of the Opera* has performed on Broadway for more than 8,000 shows.

7. After the show, stay and chat with the seniors. They'll enjoy chatting with all the stars.

Host a "Grandma and Me for Tea" Party

45

Do you remember sitting with your teddy bears and dolls to have a tea party with tiny plastic dishes? Tea parties are more fun when they involve a group of people. Get your friends together and ask them to invite their grandmothers to tea.

Here's What You'll Need

Finger foods

An assortment of teas

Cute teapots and cups (you can ask the grandmothers to bring them)

Tablecloths

Flowers for the table

Invitations

Any other things you might have at a tea party

Camera

Follow These Easy Steps

1. Have an adult help you set a day and time for the tea party. Decide on a good location that has space for the group to sit and have tea.

2. Ask a friend or two to help you make invitations. Grandmothers love homemade cards. Use colored paper and stickers and markers to write the invitations. Be sure to include all the important information: date, time, and location.

3. Make a list of the supplies you need. Can a friend bring flowers in a vase? Divide up who will bring cookies or traditional finger sandwiches. Ask someone to bring tablecloths and teapots. Have someone get a variety of teas to serve.

4. Encourage everyone to get dressed up so it seems like a formal tea. (Your grandmother probably has never seen you in a pretty dress.)

5. On the day of the tea party, allow plenty of time to get ready. If you want to be fancy, put name cards on the table.

6. Be sure to have conversation starters on the table. Write cards with questions such as "What was your favorite pet?" or "What is one story you could tell over and over again?" Some cards could ask, "What is your favorite movie and why?" or "If you could change places with one person for a day who would it be?" By having these topics on the table, you will be able to exchange stories with your grandmothers and hear about their lives growing up, as well as share your own stories.

7. Don't forget to take pictures of everyone. Then send all the grandmas a picture of this special day. Who would have thought kids can change the world by having a tea party?

You'll probably buy tea at the grocery store for the party at a reasonable price. A British tea company, PG Tips, celebrated their seventy-fifth anniversary by having a jeweler make a tea bag covered with 28 diamonds and costing more than $7,000.

Start a "Do Something" Club

46

Here's a way for you to encourage other kids to get excited about volunteering: Start a Do Something club. Do Something is an organization encouraging youth to get involved in volunteer projects. Starting a club is free and simple. There are no set-up costs, dues, or deadlines. No uniforms or adult permissions slips. Your club just has to upload two long-term projects a year to the Do Something website.

Here's What You'll Need

Supplies vary, depending on the project.

Follow These Easy Steps

1. Have an adult register to start a club on the Do Something website.

2. After you register, you'll get free pencils, posters, and bookmarks to help you publicize your club. You'll also get two hundred copies of *Build* magazine for your middle or high school. The magazine comes out three times a year. It's the only national magazine about how kids can change the world.

3. Decide on a volunteer project under the sponsorship of Do Something. Their website has a list of fundraising activities and project ideas. One Do Something club conducted a city clean-up day four years in a row. They even picked up dead animals.

4. If you need more money, apply for a $500 grant. Fill out a form describing how you'll use the money, and you might get a check.

5. On a national level, you and your leader can be part of a larger program. If a disaster happens, all Do Something club members are invited to join an emergency town meeting on IM to plan how to help. Your club has the chance to be part of the first youth response team.

Have you been involved in a major volunteer project? Apply for a BR!CK Award worth $25,000. You'll get to attend a great award ceremony with major celebrities. The BR!CK Awards is the first televised award show about making our world better. I was one of twelve finalists one year and got an all-expenses-paid trip to New York. All the information is on the Do Something website under "BR!CK Award."

Get More Information

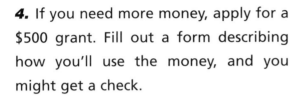 A staff member from Do Something (www.dosomething.org) is available to answer any questions you have. Just e-mail clubs@dosomething.org.

Fly Away with Airline Ambassadors

Parts of this project are expensive and require adult supervision. But who knows, maybe you can talk your parents into taking a family volunteer trip for a once-in-a-lifetime experience. Airline Ambassadors began when airline employees used their flight passes to help other people. The group would fly to a remote area and furnish an orphanage or bring supplies to a small medical clinic. Airline ambassadors escort children in need and involve youth in a variety of volunteer programs. You might find yourself working in an orphanage, teaching in a school, or helping with a feeding program. Airline Ambassadors provides a number of "tours," so people (and families) find a match with their interests to fill a need in a humanitarian project.

Here's What You'll Need

On most trips, Airline Ambassadors provides the supplies needed to carry out their projects.

If you put together an Ambassador Kit, you'll need a variety of supplies.

Follow These Easy Steps

1. Airline Ambassadors is looking for children and adults to join them on a number of upcoming Youth-2-Youth projects throughout the world. Check their website for details about the different locations.

2. If traveling to Haiti or Africa is too involved (and expensive), you have other options. Airline Ambassadors has special stay-at-home youth programs. Check out their Ambassador Kits and Cards for Kids program.

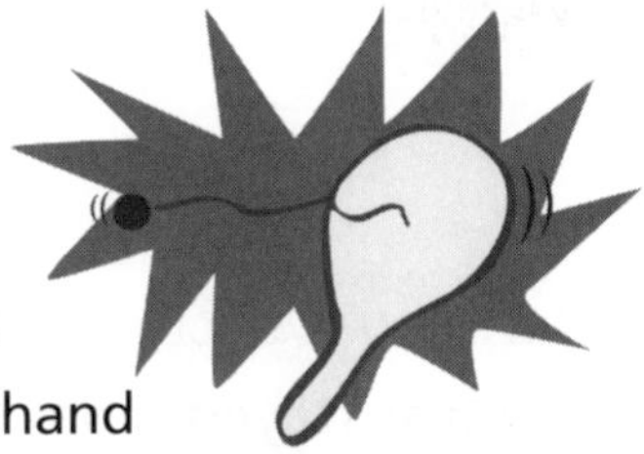

3. Airline Ambassadors asks kids to collect clothes, toys, or write holiday cards to be hand delivered to deserving people in developing countries.

4. Sign up for the youth sponsorship program and develop a personal relationship with a child in another country. Here's a sample of a typical Ambassador "School" Kit:

- Seventy-page writing tablet
- Ruler
- Safety scissors
- Colored pencils or crayons
- Two ballpoint pens
- Three pencils

5. You can put together an Ambassador Kit like this one, which is then hand delivered by an adult Airline Ambassador. They'll report back to you how your kit helped an individual child.

Airline Ambassadors has helped 500,000 people better their lives.

Get More Information

The Airline Ambassadors website (www.airlineamb.org) has everything you need to know about them.

Help Ronald McDonald

Have you ever been sick and had to go to the hospital? In most cases you just stayed a day or two. Some kids, however, have serious illnesses and need to stay in a hospital a long time. If they are in a specialty hospital, it might be far away from their home. This means parents have to stay in expensive hotels. That's where Ronald McDonald houses help. These houses are located next to major hospitals and allow parents to sleep and eat in a free, supportive environment. Ronald McDonald houses have many ways you can volunteer.

Here's What You'll Need

Supplies vary, depending on the project.

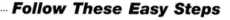

Follow These Easy Steps

1. Call the local Ronald McDonald House. Tell them how old you are and that you'd like to help. Ask what they think someone your age could do. As you talk to a staff person, you could make suggestions about how you could volunteer.

2. For example, do you like working with flowers? Many Ronald McDonald houses need volunteers to help with landscaping. You can pull weeds or plant colorful flowers.

3. How about decorating for holidays? You might have Valentine or Thanksgiving decorations you could use. Many dollar stores sell holiday decorations for one dollar.

4. Many times, brothers and sisters stay at the Ronald McDonald House. Plan a game night and bring board games so families can relax and have fun even though they're in a stressful situation.

More than 30,000 volunteers around the world donate their time at Ronald McDonald Houses.

5. Families cook their own meals at the Ronald McDonald houses, so kitchens get a lot of use. Find a quiet time to organize the pots and pans. Maybe add cute shelf paper so the cupboards look inviting.

6. Wash the windows and mirrors. It's not the most glamorous activity, but this project probably needs to be done. With so many people sharing a house, there are bound to be smudges and fingerprints on the glass. Kids can change the world one smudge at a time.

7. Tell everyone you're sponsoring a movie night. Ask your family and friends to come along and join families at the Ronald McDonald House for a night of movies and popcorn. Why not make root beer floats as a special treat?

8. Offer to sort through games, puzzles, and crayons and discard old items. It's no fun to try to do a puzzle, only to find several pieces are missing.

Get More Information

The Ronald McDonald website (www.rmhc.com) has additional information on how to volunteer.

Cut Your Hair for Locks of Love

49

Can you imagine what it would be like to go to school with a bald head because your hair had fallen out? You'd probably be shy and worried that kids would start teasing you. Locks of Love is a public nonprofit organization that provides hairpieces to financially disadvantaged children under age eighteen suffering from long-term medical hair loss. Volunteers donate hair, and a professional manufacturer assembles each custom, vacuum-fitted hairpiece. Most of the children helped by Locks of Love have lost their hair due to a medical condition called alopecia areata, which has no known cause or cure. Eighty percent of the hair donations come from kids under eighteen, so this is a great way for you to volunteer.

Here's What You'll Need

Your hair, which needs to be at least ten inches in a ponytail

Scissors

Plastic bag

Packing envelope and postage

Follow These Easy Steps

1. Make sure you are ready to cut your hair. You need to cut off at least ten inches, so this is a big decision. Make sure you have your parents' approval.

2. Wash and dry your hair.

3. Put your hair in a braid or ponytail. There must be a minimum of ten inches of hair from tip to tip in order to be used by Locks of Love. Layered hair can be used if the longest layer is ten inches. If your hair is curly, stretch it out to see if it reaches ten inches.

4. Take a deep breath, and ask an adult to cut your hair *above* the rubber band holding your ponytail.

5. Put the cut hair in a plastic bag, then a padded envelope. Do not add any hair that fell on the floor.

6. Mail the envelope to

Locks of Love
2925 10th Avenue N Suite 102
Lake Worth, FL 33461

7. If you have short hair, you can still volunteer. Ask your parent to sign up for a community partners card at Albertson's. The grocery store donates four percent of all purchases to Locks of Love. Maybe you can encourage your long-haired friends to cut their hair. Have a Locks of Love party where your friends can cut their hair as a group (with adult permission, of course). You can always have a long-term volunteer project and start growing out your hair.

> According to the *Guinness Book of World Records*, Xie Qiuping of China, has the world's longest hair; it's more than eighteen feet long. **WOW!**

Get More Information

To see pictures of children wearing wigs from donated hair, and to get more information, go to the Locks of Love website (www.locksoflove.org).

Adopt an Angel

You won't really be adopting an angel, but you can help some child or senior have a happier Christmas. The Salvation Army sponsors a nationwide program that gives gifts to children twelve and younger, as well as to needy senior citizens over the age of sixty-two. The Salvation Army learns about the children and seniors to find out if they really need help over the holidays.

This is a project you could do with your family, or if you want to help more people, get your Sunday school class, scout troop, or basketball team involved. You'll help make the holiday season special for people who don't have the things most of us take for granted.

Here's What You'll Need

A tag from an Angel Tree

Help from an adult to buy the items requested on the tag

Follow These Easy Steps

1. Beginning in the middle of November, look around for an Angel Tree. Most banks, stores, and malls have the trees in plain view. It usually is a large Christmas tree, covered with paper tags in the shape of angels.

2. After you find a tree, read the tags carefully. They will describe a person and his or her needs. For example, you might find a tag that says, "Jessica is 6 years old and would like a new doll, crayons, and a warm sweater. She is a size 7." Decide who you want to buy presents for. Do you want someone your own age? How about an elderly person living alone?

3. After selecting an Angel tag, have an adult help you buy the items on the tag. You can add a few extra items such as an age-appropriate book, warm socks, or even a new toothbrush and toothpaste.

4. Here's the important part: Make sure to read the tag to find the deadline for turning in the gifts. You usually bring the *unwrapped* presents back to the place where you got the Angel tag. If the deadline is December 12 and you don't bring your presents until December 16, the person may not get them.

5. The Salvation Army collects all the presents from the Angel Trees and brings them to a warehouse. The gifts are distributed to the people listed on the Angel tags.

During the holidays, it's fun to make some angel crafts. You can get free directions on all sorts of great projects at www.dktk-bible.com/angels.

Get More Information

In many communities, you can do an online search by typing in Angel Tree and the name of your community on the Salvation Army website (www.salvationarmy.org). Have fun shopping for a great cause.

Bring Fresh Air to a Child

If you're like most kids, you spend your summer swimming, having picnics in the park, and playing in sprinklers. It's a great time to be outside, running and playing tag with your friends. Not all kids spend their summers in the fresh air. The Fresh Air Fund Friendly Town Program gives kids in the inner city of New York a chance to experience a summer with soft grass, fresh air, and fun nature experiences. If you live in one of the thirteen Northeastern states, your family might want to host a child who normally would spend his or her summer in a tall, concrete apartment building with only a broken-down playground.

Here's What You'll Need

You need to live in a small town or suburb in one of the thirteen Northeastern states.

You need a willingness to have an inner-city child spend a week or two in your home.

Follow These Easy Steps

1. Have an adult help you see if you live in a geographical area involved with the Fresh Air Fund.

2. If you do, contact the coordinator and let him or her know you are interested in hosting a child. Children six to twelve years old stay for one to two weeks. Older children who are returning to the same family can stay longer. An adult needs to fill out paperwork.

3. You can let the Fresh Air coordinator know if you'd like a boy or girl and the general age.

The Fresh Air Fund contact will provide transportation for the child and any needed medical insurance.

4. When the child arrives, the fun starts. You don't have to do anything special. Most of these kids have never left the inner city, so seeing a grassy park with colorful playground equipment is a thrill. Do you have a lake nearby? How about a place where you can watch a cow get milked? Do you have fireflies swarming at night? All those experiences are new to your guest. One family reported their Fresh Air Fund child was scared at night because it was too quiet. He was used to sirens screeching, cars honking, and people slamming doors in his apartment building.

5. This could be an ongoing project for your family. Sixty percent of the kids in the program get invited back with the same family. Some end up staying the entire summer.

Each summer, more than 6,000 kids from New York City spend time in the country, having fun doing something as simple as picking strawberries from a backyard garden.

Get More Information

 Get everything you need on the Fresh Air Fund Friendly Town Program at their website (www.freshair.org).

Create Senior Emergency Kits

If the electricity has ever gone out at your house, you know how scary and frustrating that can be. Suddenly you can't use your TV or play video games. If it's night, you start bumping around in the dark. Ice cream starts melting in the freezer. Hopefully your parents have put together an emergency kit to get you through any problems you run into. Many seniors, however, live by themselves and aren't prepared to deal with an emergency. Your volunteer project to assemble emergency kits could help a senior get through a serious situation.

Here's What You'll Need

Resealable plastic bags

Water bottles

Flashlight

Radio

First aid kit

Extra batteries

A space blanket

Nonperishable food

Garbage bags

Anything else you think would be helpful

Follow These Easy Steps

1. Check out the American Red Cross website to see their suggestions for items to include in an emergency kit. The basic items include bottled water, a flashlight with extra batteries, first aid kit, a space blanket, and nonperishable food.

2. After you have your list of items, figure out a way to get the items. Can you do extra chores to earn the money to buy the supplies? You could write to a store to ask if they will donate items. Make sure to explain what you are doing and how it will help seniors in the community. You could ask

students in your class to help with your project and bring items from home.

3. Once you have collected all the supplies, put the items in resealable plastic bags. Clearly label each bag "EMERGENCY KIT."

4. Now that you have your packs ready, contact your local Meals on Wheels program to see if they can recommend seniors living alone who could benefit from an emergency kit. Ask a parent if you can deliver the packs yourself or if you can donate them to Meals on Wheels and have their agency distribute the bags. The next time you are stuck in a storm with the lights out, you can know you've helped at least one senior make the best of an unfortunate situation.

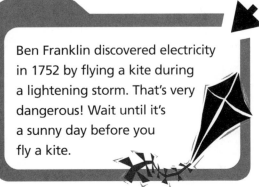

Ben Franklin discovered electricity in 1752 by flying a kite during a lightening storm. That's very dangerous! Wait until it's a sunny day before you fly a kite.

Get More Information

The American Red Cross website (www.redcross.org) gives helpful information for many emergencies.

Provide Entertainment for Children's Hospitals

When you feel sick and stay home from school, isn't it great to watch a video? It's nice to pass the time until you feel better by laughing at cartoons or a movie with your favorite characters. Most of us usually stay sick only a day or two. Think how difficult it is to pass time if you have a long hospital stay. Here's a way to help children in the hospital by collecting and donating videos and DVDs.

Here's What You'll Need

Videos and DVDs (new or used)

Transportation to video stores and to deliver the movies

Follow These Easy Steps

1. Call a local hospital and speak with the volunteer coordinator. Ask if they need videos and DVDs for the children's ward.

2. Look in the phonebook for video stores in your area. Call and talk to the manager. Yes, it's a bit scary, but people are willing to help if you have a good cause. Ask if you can set a time to meet with the manager to explain your project to donate G-rated movies to a children's hospital. Some will say yes and some will say no, but keep trying.

3. Once you have the appointment, don't be late. Ask a parent to drive you, and show up a few minutes early. You want to make a positive impression, so dress in "good" clothes (no torn jeans or faded T-shirts).

4. Before the meeting, rehearse what you'll say. Tell the manager where you plan to donate the videos. Explain how kids need to pass the time when sick. Then be bold and ask him or her to donate movies to your project. If the

> If you get a copy of the video "Wee Sing Nursery Rhymes," be sure to watch the segment with Mary and her little lamb. Our pet sheep Boomer played the role of Mary's lamb.

person says yes, thank him or her enthusiastically. If you get a no, thank the manager for agreeing to meet with you.

5. When you get home, write a thank-you note, regardless of whether the store donated movies. This keeps the doors of communication open between you and the manager. She may be so impressed you wrote a thank-you note that

she donates additional movies. Repeat this process with more local video stores.

6. Let your friends and relatives know about your video drive. They may be happy to contribute also.

7. When you have collected all the movies, take them to the hospital and donate them to the children's wing.

Support the RandomKid Water Project

When you want a drink of water, you hold a glass under the faucet in your house and get fresh, clean water. Other times you pull a water bottle out of your backpack. We take our drinking water for granted. Yet a billion people do not have access to clean, safe water, leading to the deaths of 1.5 million children under the age of five each year. The RandomKid Water Project is a way for you to raise money to bring fresh water to developing countries.

Here's What You'll Need

An organized group to work with you (such as a youth group, sports team, church, or business).

Follow These Easy Steps

1. With an adult, check out the RandomKid website for details about this program. You select a water-related project and raise funds to pay for the program.

2. You'll raise money by selling customized water bottles. With your leader, get your group to design a label, tagline, artwork, and label information. RandomKid provides templates, arranges for the labels to be made, and has the bottled water manufactured and delivered to you. They supply purified natural spring water in recyclable bottles. They are glad to share the successful marketing strategies developed by other participating groups.

3. RandomKid will cover the costs of your labeled water bottles and the shipping and freight costs. All of RandomKid services are free. Ninety percent of the sales from this project go to providing water technology to the water-stressed area

You've probably seen pictures of a traditional well where people use a hand pump to draw water in a bucket. You can use your money to buy a play pump— a children's merry-go-round attached to a water pump. As kids go round and round, they pump water into a 660-gallon water tank. See www.playpump.org for details.

that you select, and 10 percent go to their 501c3 nonprofit, RandomKid, to continue funding projects, like this one, that mobilize people to meaningfully impact others.

4. After RandomKid ships your designer water bottles, get your group to sell the water to neighbors, relatives, teachers, and anyone else who's thirsty. This will allow you to make money to fund the project you chose.

5. RandomKids is a green nonprofit. All their bottles are recyclable, and they use bottlers in your area to minimize greenhouse gasses. (Idea suggested by Talia Leman.)

Get More Information

You'll find additional details about how you can make money selling customized water bottles on the RandomKid website (www.randomkid.org/water.asp). If you have questions, contact Anne Ginther at water@randomkid.org or (214) 383-4743.

55 Help at Your Church

We forget how many people it takes to make sure all the church programs take place on a regular basis. Why not call the church office to see if you can do some volunteer work? You may end up doing boring, behind-the-scenes tasks, but they will be important, boring, behind-the-scenes tasks.

Here's What You'll Need

Most likely the church will provide any supplies.

An adult to take you to church

Follow These Easy Steps

1. Call the church office to ask if and when you can volunteer. If they have a specific job that needs doing, that's great. You also could offer suggestions. Does your church use hymnals? On a Sunday after the service, offer to turn all the hymnals facing one way so they look orderly for the service next week.

2. Many churches have weekly Bible studies or potlucks. Offer to help clean after a group meets. There's always leftover food to be put away. Even if your church has a custodian, that person will appreciate help.

3. Summer is a great time to volunteer at church. You have more free time and the church has summer activities. How about

helping with a vacation Bible school? Teachers would love to have help in working with the preschoolers.

4. Church kitchens can get disorganized because so many people use them. Offer to bring in a label maker and label where different items should go. This way, people can put things back in the right place.

5. Ask Sunday school teachers if they need help decorating bulletin boards. Use your creative touch to add borders or new pictures to a boring bulletin board.

6. Offer to fold the bulletins if the church doesn't have a folding machine. My uncle Randy goes to a men's Bible study every Saturday morning. As the men talk, they fold the church bulletins so the secretary doesn't have to do it.

I visited a church in Texas that had more than 20,000 members. The church even had a fitness center with a running track, exercise classes, and two full-time fitness teachers.

56

Go for the Glow

As usual, you want to donate money to a worthy cause. But how can you come up with money beyond your allowance and birthday (or Christmas) money? Here's another fund-raiser idea for your favorite charity. Light up your profits with glow sticks.

Here's What You'll Need

Glow bracelets, necklaces, etc.

A table

Poster board

Markers

Money box

Glow sticks

Your parent's credit card

Follow These Easy Steps

1. Have an adult help you find an event where you can sell the glow sticks. An evening event gets people excited about buying a glow stick and seeing it light at night. You can look in the paper to see about upcoming events. Is your school having a sock hop? Usually dances have dimmed lights, so glow sticks would add to the fun. Is your church hosting an evening outdoor concert? Your community's Fourth of July celebration might be a great place.

2. Once you have a date and location, make signs about your charity. People will be more likely to buy glow sticks if they know the money goes to a good cause. They may even make a donation. Don't hesitate to have a cute decorated jar with a sign saying, "Donations for Bellingham Humane Society gratefully accepted."

3. Now buy glow sticks at an inexpensive price. Don't limit yourself to glow sticks. Stores sell glow bracelets, headbands, and necklaces. Check out http://www.orientaltrading.com/ for large quantities at a reasonable cost.

4. Our local dollar store always has a large selection of glow items. Right now they're selling three glow bracelets for $1.

5. Have an adult help you figure out how many glow items you'll need. The adult probably has to place the order on a credit card, and you'll pay him or her back with your profits.

6. Make signs clearly stating the price of each glow item.

7. On the day of the event, set up a table and display your glow sticks. If the event is a large gathering of people like an outdoor concert, activate a few glow necklaces and walk through the crowd, selling your items along the way. (Have an adult come with you.) People will see your glowing decorations and will want to buy them.

8. When finished for the night, donate the money to your chosen charity and let your generous light glow.

Fireflies give off a natural glow. The eggs and larva of some fireflies glow, which is where the name *glow worms* comes from.

Get More Information

 Another place to buy glowing items is Glow Granny (www.glowgranny.com).

Give to
Oprah's Angel Network

Oprah Winfrey is known for being generous when it comes to helping people get an education or a job to improve their lives. She loves helping people and giving them tools to live more productive lives. You may not have the money Oprah has, but kids can change the world by getting involved in Oprah's Angel Network. Best of all, 100 percent of any money you donate goes directly to help the project you select. The Angel Network focuses on four main areas of need: (1) women's and children's programs, (2) education and literacy, (3) youth and community development, and (4) emergency relief. Oprah's Angel Network is dedicated to inspiring people to make a difference in the lives of others.

Here's What You'll Need

In most cases, sending a donation of money is the best way to help.

Follow These Easy Steps

1. You could select a fundraising activity from this book and send the money to Oprah's Angel Network. Here are some places your money will be used:

- In Africa parents have to pay tuition, books, and uniforms for their children to go to school. The amount isn't much (by American standards), but many parents can't afford the fees. This means their children can't attend school. Oprah has a program where you can donate money to pay for uniforms. So far, eighteen thousand kids have received uniforms through the Angel Network.

- Several years ago, Oprah visited a school with a thousand students. The school had broken windows, dirt floors, and only four toilets. Overcrowding meant some students had to sit outside and use cement blocks for desks. Now the students have a new building, a kitchen, plenty of classrooms, and a computer lab.

2. The Angel Network, in connection with Free the Children, has used money from people around the world to build schools in developing countries. They've built a vocational training center in Sri Lanka to help students get job training. The Angel Network built four schools in China and ten schools in India. By donating money, all these projects can keep growing.

As a volunteer, you might want to give money to different agencies. You can see if your money will be well spent by looking up the agency on www.charitynavigator.org. If an agency has 4 stars, that means they use their donation money wisely

Get More Information

Check out www.oprahsangelnetwork.org to get details about where to send your money to help these worthwhile programs.

Make a Difference on Make a Difference Day

58

Sometimes it's rewarding to volunteer by taking a neighbor's dog for a walk or helping the school librarian sort books. Other times, it's fun to take part in a larger volunteer project. That's where Make A Difference Day comes in. Make A Difference Day is a gigantic national day of helping others. Everyone can participate, alone or with a group. Created by *USA Weekend Magazine,* Make A Difference Day takes place on the fourth Saturday of every October. In 2006, three million people volunteered on that day. As a bonus, ten people are selected to win $10,000 each for their favorite charity. Paul Newman donates $100,000 to encourage volunteering. (You've probably eaten his spaghetti sauce or salad dressing.)

Here's What You'll Need

Supplies vary, depending on your project.

Follow These Easy Steps

1. Think about what you'd like to do on Make A Difference Day. Do you want to do a project on your own or get some friends together for a group project? Many organizations already participate in Make A Difference Day. If you belong to a scout troop, Campfire Boys and Girls, or the 4-H, check with your leader. There may be a community-wide activity planned. Then all you have to do is show up to participate.

2. Make sure the majority of your project is done on the actual Make A Difference

Day. If you are planning a canned food drive, you need to put up posters ahead of time so people know to donate. Collecting the food needs to be done on Make A Difference Day.

Actor Paul Newman has donated over $200 million to charities since 1982. He donates the profits from his food items such as spaghetti sauce, lemonade, and popcorn. When you eat his food, you're helping his volunteer projects!

The one exception is if you can't participate on Saturday because of religious reasons. In that case, do your program on Sunday.

3. Need ideas for a project? The Make A Difference Day website has an "Idea Generator" that helps you find an activity suited to your interests. They even give tips on how to contact radio stations and the newspapers so more people know about your project and can get involved.

4. Here's an important step: After your project is finished on Make A Difference Day, go to their website and fill out the entry form, describing what you did. That way the judges will include you as they look for winners to receive $10,000.

Get More Information

Make A Difference Day has a website (http://www.usaweekend.com/diffday) with lots of information about how to get involved.

Hold a Spontaneous Car Wash

How do you feel when someone does something nice for you? It's always a great feeling when you are shown unexpected kindness from a friend or family member. Volunteering can mean brightening someone's day by doing something unexpected. Something nice, that is. Do an unexpected good deed for your neighbors by washing their car.

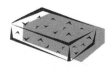

Here's What You'll Need

A bucket

Car soap

Rags or sponges

Window cleaning solution

Hose

Note cards and pen

Follow These Easy Steps

1. Check with your parents to see if it's OK to volunteer to wash a few neighbors' cars.

2. Is there someone in your neighborhood who could use a little help? Did a neighbor twist his ankle? Wash his car. Did the family next door just have a baby? Wash their car. They're probably too busy with midnight feedings to think about washing their car.

3. Gather buckets, car-washing solution, a hose, sponges, and rags. If you have a wagon, use it to carry supplies as you start on this spontaneous car wash. Get a friend or brother and sister to go with you for more fun.

4. Go to the selected neighbor's house and ring their doorbell. Surprise them by saying, "Hi, Mrs. Johnson. I know you are busy with your new baby. Jenni and I would like to help you out by washing your car. If we can hook our hose to your faucet we have everything needed to get your car clean." Mrs. Johnson will be shocked. You might have to say, "No charge—really," because people aren't used to kids doing something nice for free. She'll also be thankful for a clean car.

5. Get to work. Wet the car first, then use the soapy water and sponges to wash the car. Rinse well. Use rags and window cleaner to make the windows sparkle. As an added touch, leave a note on the windshield with a little comment such as "Enjoy your clean car. We enjoyed adding a surprise to your day."

6. For a twist on this idea, do a spontaneous car wash as a fundraiser for a charity. Go to your neighbors and offer to wash their cars for a donation. Explain which charity gets the money. People are usually happy to pay for a car wash, especially when the money goes to a good cause.

The first drive-through car wash was built in the early 1900s. Men used to push the car from station to station by hand.

Get Involved with Doing Good Together

60

Sometimes, when starting a volunteer project, it takes help from adults. Nothing wrong with that. In many cases you might start out by getting your family involved in volunteering. It's a chance to be together and have some amazing experiences as you work. The Doing Good Together organization offers suggestions for volunteer projects and lists ways to help their programs.

Here's What You'll Need

Supplies vary, depending on the project.

Follow These Easy Steps

1. Doing Good Together inspires families to volunteer. Hold a family meeting to talk about volunteering together. Your parents will be happy to have a family activity that doesn't involve a trip to the mall or playing video games. Brainstorm ideas for a volunteer project. This book has lots of ideas, as does the Doing Good Together website. If your family has never volunteered together before, start with a small project. Try some of these:

- Give your pastor and his or her spouse a gift certificate to a restaurant. Then have your family babysit their children.

- Bake cookies and take them to a local fire station to thank the firefighters for their work.
- Buy pots of colorful flowers and secretly place them on an elderly neighbor's front porch.
- Collect loose change in your house and transfer it to regular bills. Next time you go to a restaurant, surprise the waiter or waitress with an extra-big tip.

2. After your family gets comfortable volunteering in small ways, move on to a unique way of volunteering—go on a family volunteer vacation. A family vacation takes on new meaning when you volunteer and help others. One Christmas, instead of going skiing, we spent four days helping out after the Katrina disaster. Our family slept on the floor of a preschool, tore down sheetrock covered with mold, and passed out clothes to people who had lost everything in the hurricane. Those memories top any ski trip.

Check out the Doing Good Together website for a list of volunteer vacation possibilities for your family.

Get More Information

Ask your parents to look over the Doing Good Together website (www.doinggoodtogether.org). They'll probably come up with more ideas on volunteering.

Help Children Escape Child Labor

Craig Keilburger was only twelve when he began "Kids Can Free the Children," today the largest international network of children helping children. Craig was reading the comics when he read about a young boy in Pakistan named Iqbal Masih. When Iqbal was four years old, his parents sold him to a carpet weaver where he had to tie tiny knots in carpets twelve hours a day, six days a week. At twelve, Iqbal protested his working conditions and was murdered. That's when Craig decided to do something to help kids like Iqbal. Free the Children tries to stop children from being sold and working long hours under horrible conditions.

Follow These Easy Steps

1. Look at the Free the Children website. If you have questions about a project, give them a call.

2. Free the Children has built 450 schools around the world to help educate communities about the importance of sending kids to school rather than having them work in factories or fields.

Here's What You'll Need

Supplies vary, depending on your project.

3. You can collect school supplies to donate to Free the Children. One year, during the last week of school, I asked the teachers at my school if they would donate posters, workbooks, and pencils they wouldn't need.

Most teachers clean out their rooms at the end of the school year. I collected four boxes of amazing school supplies, which I sent to Africa. Ask your teachers for donations. They sometimes get free posters or books to preview.

4. Do you have a birthday coming? How about asking your family or friends to make a donation to Free the Children instead of buying you a present? Some kids having bar mitzvahs and bat mitzvahs are requesting money instead of gifts. The money is sent to Free the Children to help their programs.

5. Kids in developing countries often can't afford to see a doctor when they are sick. Collect items for health kits that Free the Children can give to schools and community centers. Simple items like bandages, antiseptic cream, gauze pads, and rubbing alcohol help take care of minor cuts and rashes.

According to Human Rights Watch 1996, India has the largest number of children in child labor. They estimate between 60 million and 115 million children work at dangerous, low-paying jobs.

INDIA

Get More Information

Read how Iqbal's story began a volunteer agency that now has more than one million members on the Free the Children website (www.freethechildren.org).

Part 5

Suggestions
for Collectors

Are you good at getting people excited about
different activities? You might be the ideal
person to collect items from other people.
Check out these ideas if you want to gather
items and donate them to help others.

62 Dress Up Dress-Up Boxes

When you were younger, did you love dressing up in costumes? Did you love putting on a cape and pretending to be a superhero, or prancing around in a sparkling tutu? Regardless, costumes are fun. I loved dressing up and using my imagination to pretend to be different characters. For little kids, dressing up is an important way of developing their imaginations. If kids live in a home where money is tight, they may not have the luxury of playing pretend in costumes. Use your imagination to decorate a dress-up box and fill it with creative outfits for a deserving child.

Here's What You'll Need

A sturdy box or plastic tub

Newspaper

Gold spray paint

Plastic jewels from the craft store

Glue

Dress-up clothes

Follow These Easy Steps

1. Have an adult help you call a few places like the Boys and Girls Club or Head Start program and ask if they would like a dress-up box filled with cool costumes. You'll soon find someone who is excited about getting your gift.

2. One of the fun things about playing dress-up is to have a creative storage box. Set your sturdy box or plastic container on old newspaper outside. Lightly spray the box with gold spray paint. Let it dry and paint it again. Glue on the jewels to give the box a "fancy" effect.

3. Look through your own dress-up box and see if there are costumes you don't need anymore. Ask your friends and family if they have extra dress-up items. Most people are happy to donate hats, sparkly tops, and colorful scarves for your dress-up box.

4. Ask your parents to take you to garage sales and thrift stores. Try to find items boys would use also. Many times thrift shops sell construction hats or medical uniforms. You might find a simple piece of shiny fabric that kids can use in all sorts of creative ways.

5. Make sure all the costumes are clean and in good condition before putting them in the dress-up box.

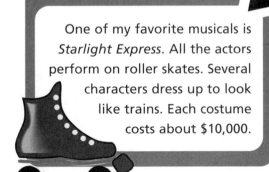

One of my favorite musicals is *Starlight Express*. All the actors perform on roller skates. Several characters dress up to look like trains. Each costume costs about $10,000.

6. Take the dress-up box to the agency you selected. Your gift is guaranteed to bring hours of creative fun to other kids.

Recycle Bibles

Since the Bible is the number one best-selling book, you probably have a few in your house. I got my first picture Bible as a two-year-old and even owned a Bible written like a comic strip. You probably have at least one Bible in your house, even if you don't attend church regularly. We take it for granted to be able to buy and read a Bible any time we want. In many parts of the world, people are persecuted for owning a Bible. The Bible League will send your extra Bibles to thousands of people around the world who could never get a Bible on their own.

Here's What You'll Need

An assortment of Bibles

Colorful collection boxes

Boxes for shipping

Packing tape

Money to pay for shipping

Follow These Easy Steps

1. This project is pretty basic—collect Bibles. The Bible League asks you to send Bibles with the Old and New Testaments. They can't use Bibles containing only New Testaments or portions of Bibles. Children's Bibles are gratefully accepted.

2. Ask your parents' help to go through the house and collect Bibles gathering dust. Maybe you have children's Bibles you've outgrown.

3. Call relatives, asking them to donate unused Bibles. Many people have more than one Bible, so they can do a good deed and donate one to a needy person.

4. If you attend church, ask the pastor for help with your project. He or she might let you make an announcement, asking church members to bring in extra Bibles. Let people know you'll have a colorful collection box by the front door for easy Bible drop-off. Don't be shy. Ask people to make a cash donation if they don't have extra Bibles. You'll use the money to ship the Bibles to the Bible League's warehouse.

5. Here's an unusual way to collect Bibles. Ask your pastor if you can have the Bibles left in the church lost and found box. You'll be amazed how many people leave their Bibles at church and never look for them. Did you ever think kids can change the world by getting Bibles from the lost and found?

6. After you've collected the Bibles, pack them in sturdy boxes and ship them to

> Bible League Warehouse
> 15925 Van Drunen Road
> South Holland, IL 60473

The Bible has been translated into more than 2,018 languages.

7. Make sure to write "MEDIA MAIL" in big letters on the box. That gets you a cheaper rate if you are shipping with the US Post Office.

Get More Information

Find out about other volunteer opportunities with the Bible League on their website (www.bibleleague.org). In 2006 the Bible League placed 17 million Bibles. It costs 75¢ to ship and distribute a used Bible, compared to $4 to print, ship, and distribute a new Bible.

Swap Books

Do you have extra books under your bed and stuffed into your bookcase? Do you love to read books but don't want to spend the money to buy new ones all the time? Have a book swap. It's a great way to recycle old books and get new ones you haven't read yet.

Here's What You'll Need

Location for the swap

Small poker chips or paper tickets

Flyers for publicity

Table to display books

Signs saying "mystery," "adventure," "non-fiction," etc.

Follow These Easy Steps

1. Have an adult help you select a location and a time for the event. Sometimes libraries have community rooms they let you use free. If you have a large garage or basement, that might work.

2. Print some flyers to give to your friends and neighbors with all the important information. Explain that the book swap is a one-on-one exchange. If they bring ten books, they can get ten different books. People also can donate books.

3. An easy way to run this event is to set a drop-off time for the books. For example, people can donate books from 2–2:30 p.m. If someone brings five books, they get five credits in the form of five poker chips or tickets. Then they wait outside until the 2:30 opening time.

4. Put signs on the tables with labels such as "mystery" and "adventure."

5. Have help ready to put the donated books on the labeled tables as soon as they are dropped off. When people come to the swap, they can glance at the signs on the tables and easily find Nancy Drew books or look for a new adventure story.

6. At your designated starting time, open the doors and let people come in and select their "new" books. They can get as many books as they have tokens for. Make sure you have several people as "cashiers." They stand at the check-out table and collect tokens from your customers.

7. After the event, box any extra books and take them to the Salvation Army or Goodwill. That way they have another chance of being recycled. Go home and relax by reading one of your "new" books.

You'll be amazed at the wide variety of books people bring to your book swap. In 2006 there were 291,920 different titles published!

Collect Pajamas

It's always great at the end of a busy day to be able to slip into your comfy pajamas and have an adult read you a bedtime story. You probably haven't thought about the fact that many children don't even own pajamas. If a child comes from a low-income family, parents struggle to provide daytime clothes. Pajamas are a luxury. You can help by collecting PJs and donating them to the national Pajama Program. Their goal is to provide new, warm pajamas and books to children in need.

Here's What You'll Need

New pajamas

Collection boxes or tubs (optional)

Flyers or posters (optional)

Follow These Easy Steps

1. Check out the Pajama Program website to see if a local chapter is in your community. Contact the director and let him or her know about your plans to participate.

2. Decide on a way to collect new pajamas. How about having a sleepover where you and your friends play games and have fun in your pajamas? Of course you'll ask your friends to bring new pajamas to the party.

3. Enlist the help of your church or your school. Make flyers and put them up to encourage people to donate children's pajamas. Be sure to tell people the pajamas

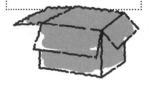

will be sent to kids in places like the Ukraine, South Africa, and inner-city children in the United States.

4. Place boxes or tubs in convenient places where people can drop off their donations. Usually you can do a drive for a week, so people have several chances to bring the pajamas. Clearly label boxes or crates, so people know where to put donations.

5. Once you have collected the pajamas, pack them in sturdy boxes. Your local Pajama Program coordinator will tell you where to ship them for distribution.

6. If you want to give out pajamas in your community, call a local women and children's shelter to see if they can use your pajama donations. If so, arrange a time to have an adult help you drop off the PJs.

7. Now when you slip into your pajamas to go to bed, you can know that other kids around the world are doing the same thing.

Did you know April 16 is National Pajama Day? It's the day after your parents have to turn in their taxes. This is a day they probably want to relax.

APRIL 16

Get More Information

The Pajama Program has local chapters in many states and overseas. Find the nearest location by looking on their website (www.pajamaprogram.org).

Help Heavenly Hats

How do you feel when you're having a bad hair day? Do you just want to grab the next scarf or hat to cover your hair disaster? I always feel self-conscious when my hair is sticking up in weird places. People with cancer often have to deal with losing their hair due to the medications they take. You can help by donating new hats to people who have lost their hair. The Heavenly Hats Foundation collects and distributes new hats to those heroes of all ages who lose their hair due to the treatment of cancer or other medical conditions. The Heavenly Hats Foundation was founded by teenager Anthony Leanna when he was ten years old.

Here's What You'll Need

New hats

Shipping boxes

Money to pay for postage

Follow These Easy Steps

1. Think of ways to collect new hats. The hats have to be new to make sure there are no germs. Many of the people getting these hats have a weakened immune system and can easily get sick. Ask your parents if they will take you to buy a new hat. Grandparents are always willing to help their grandkids. See if Grandma or Grandpa will take you shopping for a few cute hats to donate. Maybe you can do extra chores around the house to have extra money to buy hats.

2. On a bigger scale, you could do a drive to collect hats. Get your class or your school involved. Ask a teacher if you can talk about the program in front of the class for a few minutes. Make sure people understand the hats have to be lightweight and new.

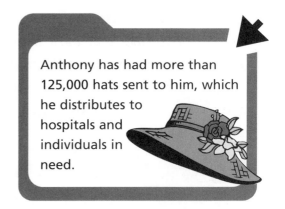

Anthony has had more than 125,000 hats sent to him, which he distributes to hospitals and individuals in need.

3. Once you have collected or bought the hats, pack them up and send to

Anthony D. Leanna
2325 Pamperin Rd. Suite 3
Green Bay, WI 54313

Get More Information

Check out www.heavenlyhats.com for more information on this great program.

67 Glue Down Those Coins

Many groups collect change to raise money for a cause. People donate loose change; all those pennies, dimes, and quarters add up. Try this fun way to get people excited about bringing in change.

Here's What You'll Need

Large pieces of butcher paper or cardboard

Lots of glue

Coins

Paper and markers for posters

Follow These Easy Steps

1. Find an organization or cause you want to help. As with all fundraising programs, people want to know where their money is going. It's too vague to say, "The coins go to help poor people." Instead, let people know, "The money goes to help the Johnson family at our school because their house burned down."

2. Ask your teacher or principal if this can be a school project. The more people involved, the more change you'll collect.

3. Come up with a symbol to represent your cause. When I did this, I was raising money to help kids in Africa pay for their tuition. I drew an outline of Africa on huge sheets of paper. Are you raising money to buy dog food for an animal shelter? How about drawing a picture of a dog or cat?

4. Let people know what day you are doing the project. They'll need a few days to collect loose change from their houses and car cup holders.

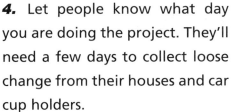

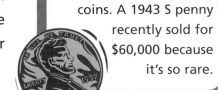

Check the dates on your coins. A 1943 S penny recently sold for $60,000 because it's so rare.

5. On collection day make sure you have the paper outlines on the floor. Place bottles of glue all around. If you have a large group, make several outlines on paper and place them around the room. Put up signs saying things like, "Bring in loose change and help us fill this map of Africa with coins."

6. Here's the fun part. Have people glue coins on the outline of your fundraising symbol. When the outline is covered with coins, start filling in the entire shape. It's fun to see how the pieces of cardboard and paper get covered with coins.

7. Be sure to keep the coin-filled papers on display for a few days. People like looking at the result of their efforts.

8. OK, now comes the hard part. You have to get the coins off the paper and into a bank or coin counting machine. Get a friend to help you peel off the coins. Most of the time they pop right off. If a coin has tiny pieces of paper glued to it, drop the coin into a bucket of warm water. The paper quickly peels off.

9. When all the coins are off the paper, have an adult take you to the bank or a coin sorting machine. Get a check for the amount and donate it to the designated charity.

10. Be sure to let your school know how much money they helped collect.

68 Prepare Mini Hygiene Kits

I have at least five different shampoos and conditioners in my shower at home. Then, of course, there's my toothpaste, mouthwash, and an assortment of great-smelling soaps cluttering my bathroom sink. Most of us take it for granted we'll always have soap and shampoo. Yet homeless people often don't have the most basic items to keep clean. A recent article in our paper described a homeless man who washed his face in a fountain because he didn't have any other place to get clean. Here's a way to put together small hygiene bags for people who need them.

Here's What You'll Need

Small resealable plastic bags

Individual bottles of shampoo, bars of soap, toothpaste, etc.

Follow These Easy Steps

1. Have an adult help you call a homeless shelter or women's shelter to ask if they can use hygiene kits filled with soap and shampoo.

2. The next time you are on vacation or stay in a hotel, ask your parents if you can take the little bottles of shampoo and conditioner and wrapped soaps home. Hotels usually have several bars of soap available. (In case you're wondering whether this is stealing, most hotel chains plan for their guests to take things that start with the letter S: soap, shampoo, shower caps, shower gels, slippers, and so forth. It's OK to take these from your room, but it's never OK to take them from the maids' cart.) Our family uses one, and we take the unopened bars with us to donate.

3. As your parents pay when you're checking out of the hotel, ask the employee if they would donate some additional soaps and shampoos for your project. I did this once, and the hotel donated 144 toothbrushes.

4. Ask your friends and neighbors to check their bathrooms for the soaps and shampoos they've brought home from hotels.

5. Make an announcement at your school or church before a major holiday like Christmas or spring break. Encourage people to collect hygiene items from hotels as they travel.

6. Ask your parents for help buying toothbrushes and toothpaste. Dollar stores often sell three toothbrushes for $1.

7. When you have an assortment of items, place them in the resealable bag. It's great if each bag has a new bar of soap, bottle of shampoo, a new toothbrush, and a small tube of toothpaste.

8. Have an adult take you to the homeless shelter to make your donation.

My mom has a variation on this idea. Many homeless people have pets with them. She used to put dog biscuits in a plastic bag and give them to homeless people as a special treat for their dog. Make sure you have adult approval to do this volunteer activity.

Tap into a Dance Shoe Drive

69

There is something magical about the sound of tap shoes on a dance studio floor. But where do those taps go when you grow out of them? What can you do with pink leather ballet shoes too small for your feet? Share the magic of dance by sponsoring a dance shoe drive. Many agencies working with children could use the shoes to expand their dance programs.

Here's What You'll Need

Large boxes or tubs

Markers and poster board

Follow These Easy Steps

1. Have an adult help you call a local Boys and Girls Club or Big Brothers Big Sisters program. These agencies work with low-income children. Ask if they can use donations of dance shoes for their programs. Often they sponsor dance classes and know about kids needing dance shoes. If you collect dance shoes in smaller sizes, contact a Head Start program. These early-childhood schools would love dance shoes for their preschool students to use in dress-up play.

2. Talk to the director of your dance studio to ask for his or her permission to do the drive. Discuss the best way to ask for shoe donations. Is there an e-mail list you could send a message out on? (Make sure to have the director proofread it first). Perhaps you can print flyers giving details on the dance shoe drive. Decorate boxes or tubs with signs that say "Drop Off Used Dance Shoes Here."

3. Make posters using bright-colored markers. Post them around the studio. Let people know the dates of the shoe drive and to deposit their shoes in the decorated boxes you provide. Ask people to put a rubber band or tie a string around each pair of shoes. Otherwise you'll have loose shoes everywhere. After the collection date, sort the shoes to make sure they are all in good condition. Ask an adult to drive you to the agency receiving the shoes.

A professional ballerina *en pointe* (standing on her toes) wears out a pair of pointe shoes (sometimes called "toe" shoes) in eight to twelve hours.

Collect School Supplies for Kids

One of my favorite things about starting school in the fall is getting new pens, pencils, notebooks, and binders. It's nice to have new supplies to start the year with a clean slate. But not everyone has the money to buy these items. You can help by buying and collecting extra school supplies to donate to children in need.

Here's What You'll Need

Supplies like markers, paper, notebooks, binders, pens, pencils, calculators, folders, dividers, etc.

Collection boxes or bins

Follow These Easy Steps

1. Call your school principal to ask if there are kids at your school who might have trouble buying new school supplies. If there are, offer to bring in items your principal can distribute. He or she knows how to give the supplies so kids don't feel bad about not having money to buy their own. In the event students at your school don't need donated supplies, your principal will be able to give you the name of another school to contact.

2. Ask your parents if they would be willing to buy extra school supplies for kids who don't have as much. Offer to do extra chores around the house to earn more money to buy the school supplies.

3. Check your newspaper for sales. A store down the street from my house is selling spiral notebooks for ten cents each. You can help your money go a long way by looking for bargains.

4. Call a few friends or members of your soccer team. Ask them to ask their parents to buy a few extra items when school shopping. Most parents don't mind buying some new pencils or an extra bottle of glue when it's going to a good cause.

5. When you go with an adult to buy your supplies, ask to talk to the store manager. Explain your plan to donate school items to your principal. See if the store is willing to make a contribution.

6. Another option is to ask the store manager if you can leave a decorated donation box at the front of the store. Add a big sign that says, "Please Donate Extra School Supplies to Children at Silver Lake Elementary School." Customers will purchase paper, markers, scissors, and other supplies and drop them in the box.

7. Before school starts, collect all the supplies and give them all to your school principal.

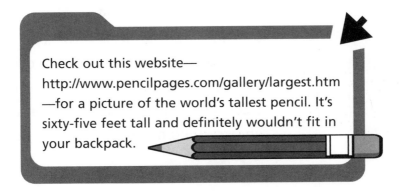

Check out this website—
http://www.pencilpages.com/gallery/largest.htm
—for a picture of the world's tallest pencil. It's sixty-five feet tall and definitely wouldn't fit in your backpack.

Score with a Sports Equipment Drive

71

Do you have unused soccer balls, baseball bats, gloves, in-line skates, or basketballs around your house and garage? Not all kids have the money to buy sports equipment. Sponsor a drive to collect sports equipment to donate to a Boys and Girls Club or other organization for underprivileged kids.

Here's What You'll Need

Collection bins
Poster board
Markers

Follow These Easy Steps

1. Find an agency that could use the sports equipment. Call the Salvation Army, Big Brothers Big Sisters, or Boys and Girls Clubs to ask if they want the sports equipment.

2. Find a group of people to help collect the sports equipment. What about the sports teams at your school? Pick a group of people who would be willing to donate and collect the balls, bats, shoes, and more.

3. Design and print flyers to pass out at sporting events, school, or church to publicize your event and your collection bin locations. Be sure to state that all sports equipment should be clean and in good condition.

4. On the day or week of the collection, put labels on the bins so people can see where to put the sports equipment. Add balloons or streamers. If you have one central drop-off location, try to be there when most people will be dropping off items. Thank people for helping.

5. Once you have collected all the equipment, inspect everything to make sure it's in good shape. No one wants to get a donated soccer ball that leaks. Wipe off the shoes, inflate all the balls, and check for rips and tears.

6. With your parent's help, deliver the donated items to your selected agency. You'll be giving kids the chance to exercise and experience the joy of playing sports.

Soccer is the most played and most watched sport on Earth.

72 Round up Extra Shoes

Take a glance through the closets in your house. I'm sure you and the rest of your family have lots of shoes—tennis shoes, dress-up shoes, sandals, boots, and flip-flops. Have you ever thought that your shoes protect you from disease? Millions of people don't have shoes to protect their feet from diseases or bacteria. A cut on the foot can lead to a serious infection. Here's an easy project to help. Soles4Souls helps people around the world get a pair of shoes and a chance to have a healthier life.

Here's What You'll Need

Boxes or bags to collect the shoes

Crayons, markers, and paper to decorate the boxes

Heavy-duty rubber bands

Flyers or posters (optional)

Shipping boxes

Money to pay for shipping

Packing tape

Follow These Easy Steps

1. Begin by going through your own closet and collecting "gently worn" shoes. Place each pair of shoes sole to sole, and hold them together with a rubber band.

2. Brainstorm with your family and friends how you can collect more shoes. Do you belong to a soccer team? What about your dance class? Maybe your scout troop is interested in helping. Ask a leader at your church for help. Schools can have competitions between classes to see who can bring in the most shoes. Call relatives and tell them about your project.

3. After you've decided who to ask for shoes, you could make some flyers or posters. List all the important information like this:

People in Kenya need your shoes. Please clean out your closets and donate new or gently used shoes. Bring shoes to church on Sunday, June 15. Shoes will be sent to a school in Kenya and given to students and staff who don't have shoes. If you can't donate shoes, we'll gladly take donations to pay for shipping.

4. Pass out the flyers and put up posters to remind people when and where to bring shoes.

5. Have decorated boxes available to collect the shoes. Be sure to put a rubber band around each pair.

6. Have an adult help you pack all the collected shoes in sturdy boxes and ship to Souls4Soles warehouse in Alabama or Nevada, whichever is closest

Soles4Souls, Inc.
315 Airport Road
Roanoke, AL 36274

Soles4Souls, Inc., Foreign
Trade Zone #89
6620 Escondido Street
Las Vegas, Nevada 89119

Soles4Souls gives away one pair of shoes every twenty-eight seconds.

7. They will sort the shoes and get them to orphanages, flood or disaster victims, and other needy people.

Get More Information

Check out the Soles4Souls website (www.soles4souls.org) for a map of all the places they ship donated shoes.

Give Stuffed Animals to Offer Comfort

73

Firefighters and police officers often deal with kids going through sad experiences. Stuffed animals can comfort a child who had her house burn down or was involved in a car accident. By collecting stuffed animals you'll make a scary situation a little less stressful for a child.

Here's What You'll Need

Several collection boxes

Colorful ribbons or bows (optional)

New or nearly new stuffed animals

Signs that read "Donate New or Gently Used Stuffed Animals to our Local Fire and Police Department"

Follow These Easy Steps

1. Contact your local fire or police station to see if they accept donations of stuffed animals. They may request only small animals or require the stuffed animals be brand new.

2. Contact friends and relatives to see if they have stuffed animals you could have for your drive. Tell them how the animals are going to be used. You may even have a relative with a giant collection of unused Beanie Babies.

3. Ask your principal or pastor if you can place collection boxes around so people can drop off donations. Maybe your mom or dad could take a collection box to their workplace so employees have a chance to donate. Let people know the last day to drop off animals.

4. Once you've collected all the animals, as an added touch, tie bows around each animal's neck or middle.

Want to see pictures of teddy bears or stuffed animals? Look at www.agapebears.com for 5,000 pictures of stuffed animals.

5. Call the police station or fire department and find a good time for you to deliver your furry critters. Have an adult help you drop off the items. (This activity was suggested by Hannah Bonestroo.)

Pack Up Backpacks for Foster Kids

Think about the last time you had a sleepover at a friend's house. You probably stuffed a backpack or duffle bag with pajamas, extra clothes, and your favorite stuffed animal. Now think what it would be like to be a foster child, having to move from one home to the next because your parents aren't able to take care of you. Some foster kids are taken from their homes without time to pack a suitcase. They sometimes arrive at a new foster home with a few items in a paper grocery bag.

Help foster children by collecting backpacks and small suitcases to give them as they move to a new home.

Here's What You'll Need

Backpacks and small suitcases

Small toy like you would get in fast-food kids' meals (optional)

Follow These Easy Steps

1. Have an adult call your local Department of Social Services or Child Protective Services. Those departments can connect you to people involved with foster children. Explain what you want to do. After they agree they can use the backpacks, get to work.

2. Think of creative ways to collect backpacks. Here are some suggestions:

- Write letters to the managers of stores such as Wal-Mart, K-Mart, and other stores selling backpacks.

Describe your plan to collect backpacks for kids in foster care so they can carry basic things with them. Ask them to make a donation to your cause. If you don't hear from the managers in a few weeks, call back. They'll be surprised a kid is so persistent.

- Ask local schools if you can have the backpacks from their lost and found boxes. Many schools donate all the items to charity anyway. I once got fifteen coats and twenty-two sweatshirts from my school's lost and found, which I sent to Africa.

- In the summer spread the word you are collecting backpacks. Many kids get new backpacks for the upcoming school year, and you can collect the used ones.

- Go through your house to see how many extra backpacks, duffle bags, and small suitcases you have.

3. After you've collected the items, check them to make sure they are clean and in good shape. If possible, add a small stuffed animal or toy as a special treat.

4. Have an adult help you deliver the backpacks to the foster-care agency you contacted.

Some kids are getting backaches from carrying backpacks filled with notebooks and books. Doctors say your backpack should never be heavier than 10 percent of your weight.

Gather Hats for Homeless People

When it's cold outside, the only thing I want to do is bundle in a sweater, throw on my wool socks, and curl up by the fire with a cup of hot cocoa. While I have the opportunity to stay warm, not everyone has a fireplace or a hat to wear outside. Help needy people keep warm in the winter by collecting new or gently used hats, scarves, and gloves to donate to your local homeless shelter.

Here's What You'll Need

Poster board

Flyers

Markers

Cardboard boxes

Follow These Easy Steps

1. Get in touch with an agency in town that works with low-income or homeless people. Ask if they can use winter hats, gloves, and scarves. They'll give you specific information so you don't collect the wrong items.

2. Designate a place where your collection boxes will be located. People want to know they can easily drop off the items.

3. Brainstorm with an adult how you can collect the winter items. Send e-mails to friends and relatives, asking them to donate. Set a specific date to collect the items. Make flyers to give to your youth group, soccer team, or scouting group.

Ask your principal if the collection drive can be a school project. Just think how many items you could collect if all the students in your school contributed.

4. Make posters describing your volunteer project. Post them wherever there are community bulletin boards (at libraries, family restaurants, and grocery stores).

5. Call the local paper and tell them what you are doing. They might write an article about you and your project. That way even more people can bring donations.

6. After you've collected the items, sort through them to make sure they are in good condition. Have an adult drive you to the charity to drop off all your warm items.

On January 23, 1971, the temperature in Prospect Creek, Alaska, dropped to -80 degrees. You'd need to wear several hats in that weather.

Collect Cell Phones for People in Need

76

While you may not drive yet, I always feel safer when I have my phone as I drive from place to place. A few months ago I got in a tiny accident, and it was good to be able to call my dad right away. Yet cell phones are costly, and the monthly fee is expensive. It's sad to think some women living in dangerous situations or seniors living alone can't afford to have a cell phone when they need it to call 911. You can help by collecting old cell phones and donating them to a woman's shelter or senior center.

Here's What You'll Need

Old cell phones

Collection boxes or bins

Posters and flyers

Follow These Easy Steps

1. Contact a local women's shelter or senior center to ask if they want used cell phones that can be used to call 911. Each organization has different needs. If they say yes, start collecting cell phones and arrange to make a donation.

2. Here's another option. An agency called Cell Phones for Life has an interesting way to help people get the cell phones they need. They sponsor shelters and agencies that serve the elderly and battered women. Many shelters have cell phones donated to them but do not have time to refurbish and test each donated phone. Cell Phones for Life helps organizations by giving away free emergency-use cell phones. There is no cost to receive or use them. Phones donated can be reconditioned and distributed back to your community free of charge.

3. Start spreading the word that you are collecting used cell phones. Can you speak at your church on a Sunday morning? Ask a parent to let co-workers know about your plans. Pass out flyers at your next sports match. Ask teachers at your school to donate used phones. Most adults quickly say, "I have an old cell phone stuck in a drawer I'd be glad to donate."

4. If you have six or more phones, Cell Phones for Life will send UPS to pick them up free. After you finish collecting the cell phones, call Cell Phones for Life about shipping details.

Have you asked your parents for a cell phone, but they said it was too expensive? Luxury accessory producer Peter Aloisson has created the Diamond Crypto Smartphone priced at $1.3 million. It's covered with 50 diamonds and 18-carat rose gold.

Get More Information

The website www.cellphonesforlife.org gives all the information you need to run a cell phone collection drive. You'll feel good knowing that because of your effort, some person in need will be able to call 911 in an emergency.

Participate in the Pasta for Pennies Program

Does your family have a "change jar" where your mom and dad toss change from their pockets at the end of the day? Would you find loose pennies and dimes under your couch cushions? Most homes have coins scattered around drawers, under car seats, and in the bottom of backpacks. Often we say, "Oh, it's just a few pennies," but those pennies add up. Olive Garden Restaurant has a program called Pasta for Pennies that encourages people to collect coins as a fund-raiser for the Leukemia and Lymphoma Society. In 2006 the program collected $4.2 million.

Here's What You'll Need

Lots of coins

Collection containers for the coin envelopes

Adult support

Follow These Easy Steps

1. Pasta for Pennies is designed as a school project, so you'll need to get your teacher and principal involved. That shouldn't be hard, since they'll see this as an easy volunteer project that makes a big impact. There is also a chance for your school to win prizes. Olive Garden Restaurant offers a Hospitaliano Pasta Party lunch to the class at each school raising the most money. Other prizes include computers and sports equipment.

2. Have an adult register your school at www.schoolandyouth.org/school/Controller. You'll receive flyers, information, and envelopes to give all the students at your school to collect coins.

3. In many cases Pasta for Pennies will give you the name of a person with leukemia or lymphoma in your area. All the money is raised in that person's honor. (You might have someone at your school with one of these diseases.)

4. The coin drive runs for three weeks from late February to early March. During that time, come up with different competitions to encourage kids to bring in coins. How about having a scale and weigh each class's coins? On another day, have coin stacking contests to see who can stack quarters the highest. Have each class lay coins end to end in the gym and see which class makes the longest line of coins.

5. At the end of the three weeks, help teachers collect the coin envelopes. Get the coins counted at a bank and send a check to the Leukemia Society for that amount. Don't send them the loose coins.

Americans have been using pennies since 1793. If you want more information about coins, check out www.coinsite.com. You can ask the Coin Doc any coin-related question.

Get More Information

Pasta for Pennies is cosponsored with Olive Garden and the School and Youth Program Division of the Leukemia and Lymphoma Society. Call (212) 689-1400 ext. 261 for information.

Index

Extra Easy Volunteer Projects

Adopt an Angel 114

Build-A-Bear Workshop 52

Clean Baby Drool 94

Design Funky Umbrellas 50

Fill Bedtime Snack Sacks 48

Give Away Easter Baskets 28

Help Dogs Avoid Heatstroke 22

Hold a Spontaneous Car Wash 132

Host a "Grandma and Me for Tea" Party 104

Locks of Love 112

More Than Warmth 42

No-Sew Fleece Blankets 36

Raise Funds with Dinosaur-Teeth Necklaces 54

Recycle at Home 68

Sell "Diamond" Pins 46

Take a Dog for a Walk 20

Use Pen-and-Paper Power 86

Wear Jeans for a Cause 100

Fundraising Ideas

Design Funky Umbrellas 50

Glue Down Those Coins 150

Go for the Glow 126

GospelShoe 82

Great American Bake Sale 32

Pasta for Pennies 170

Raise Funds with Dinosaur-Teeth Necklaces 54

RandomKid Water Project 122

Recycle with a Recycling Carnival 58

Sell "Diamond" Pins 46

Wear Jeans for a Cause 100

Wrap for Charity 34

Volunteering to Help Other Kids

Adopt an Angel 114

Build-A-Bear Workshop 52

Collect School Supplies for Kids 156

Decorate and Fill Art Bags for Ill Children 30

Dress Up Dress-Up Boxes 140

Fill Bedtime Snack Sacks 48

Free the Children 136

Fresh Air Fund 116

Give Away Easter Baskets 28

Give Giggle Bags 40

Kids for Kids 98

Locks of Love 112

Pack Up Backpacks for Foster Kids 164

Pajama Program 146

Prepare Birthday Bags for Children Living in Shelters 38

Provide Entertainment for Children's Hospitals 120

Ronald McDonald House 110

Royal Family Kids' Camp 90

Score with a Sports Equipment Drive 158

Soles4Souls 160

Tap into a Dance Shoe Drive 154

World Hope International 80

Working with Established Organizations

Adopt an Angel 114

Airline Ambassadors 108

Bible League 142

Build-A-Bear Workshop 52

Cell Phones for Life 168

Childcare Worldwide 98

Do Something 106

Doing Good Together 134

Free the Children 136

Fresh Air Fund 116

GospelShoe 82

Great American Bake Sale 32

Guide Dogs for the Blind 18

Habitat for Humanity 44

Heavenly Hats 148

Heifer International 14

Humane Society of the United States 20

Kids F.A.C.E. 64

Kids For Kids 98

Kids Saving the Rain Forest 60

Locks of Love 112

Make A Difference Day 130

Meals on Wheels 118

More Than Warmth 42

National Arbor Day Foundation 62

National Recreation and Park Association 76

National Wildlife Federation 12

Oprah's Angel Network 128

Pajama Program 146

Passport in Time 70

Pasta for Pennies 170

RandomKid Water Project 122

Ronald McDonald House 110

Roots and Shoots 24

Royal Family Kids' Camp 90

Soles4Souls 160

Special Olympics 92

USDA Forest Service 74

World Hope International 80

Volunteer

I hope you've gotten ideas on how to volunteer in this book. Here are a few more ideas to spark your imagination and get you involved in a program. Just think about these when you see the word VOLUNTEER.

V—Very few people can turn down helping a kid doing a volunteer project. Don't be afraid to ask adults to donate their time, money, or supplies. Grownups love seeing kids involved in worthwhile activities.

O—Opportunities to volunteer are everywhere. Don't feel you need to start a nationwide campaign to save the planet. You can volunteer on a smaller basis and still make a difference.

L—Look in your local newspaper for ideas on volunteering. Many papers have sections called "Volunteer Opportunities." Check out the list and see how to help.

U—Unless you take action, your volunteer project never gets going. It's easy to say, "I wish I could help animals." It takes effort to find a need and start working toward filling that need.

N—Never let anyone tell you you're too young. Kids can change the world. My friend Gabby Fee was six years old when she put together birthday bags for kids in a homeless shelter. Find an age-appropriate project and get going.

T—Try something new. That's what's great about volunteering: You can experiment. Maybe you're shy. Take a risk and give a short speech to your Sunday school class about your project.

E—Encourage others to volunteer. If you're excited, they will be also. Invite friends to help with your project.

E—Experiment with different volunteer projects. You may think you love working outside and clearing trails at a park. Then you get there and find bugs, dirt, and too much work. Don't give up on volunteering. Find another activity like doing crafts with preschoolers or walking dogs.

R—Research different opportunities. Talk to friends who volunteer or read books on the subject. If you like working with the environment, call a few environmental places and see what they have to offer. You might love to volunteer at the zoo, but find out you have to be eighteen. Don't get discouraged. Keep checking out opportunities until you find the perfect project for you.

Happy volunteering!